ELITE

PERFORMANCE
FOR MANAGERS

WWW.EXECPATHFINDERS.COM

Exec Pathfinders LLC

"Begin with the end in mind"

Elite Performance Pillars™
Los Angeles | London

COPYRIGHT © 2024 TALBOT ALLEN STARK
Published by Elite Performance Pillars™, a division of ExecPathfinders Publishing

ISBN
eBook: 979-8-9895434-0-3
Paperback: 979-8-9895434-1-0
Hardcover: 979-8-9895434-2-7

Library of Congress Control Number: 2023921666

First Edition
Book Production and Publishing by *Brands Through Books*

brandsthroughbooks.com

The scripture cited in the segment "A Note to the Reader" is taken from the New King James Version®. Copyright © 1982 by Thomas Nelson. Used by permission. All rights reserved.
Other scripture cited within the text is taken from The Holy Bible, New International Version®, NIV®, Copyright©, 1973, 1978, 1984, 2011 by Biblica, Inc. Used by permission. All rights reserved worldwide.

ExecPathfinders.com

ELITE

PERFORMANCE
FOR MANAGERS

The Essential Steps for Transforming
Your Career, Life, and Destiny

TALBOT A. STARK

ExecPathfinders Publishing
A Division of Elite Performance Pillars™

Elite Performance for Managers is a career game changer. It doesn't just promise to elevate your career; it delivers on that promise. This book will revolutionize your perspective on your professional journey, offering a step-by-step roadmap to transform you into a highly effective career manager. What sets Talbot's book apart is its actionable approach. With clear guidance and practical tactics, you can immediately start crafting the career you've always dreamed of. From setting ambitious goals to navigating the twists and turns of your career path, this book empowers you every step of the way.

—KEN BURKE, founder of MarketLive, CEO of Microcasting, Inc., and author of *Intelligent Selling: The Art and Science of Selling Online* and *Prosper: Five Steps to Thriving in Business and Life*

Elite Performance for Managers provides a tactical advantage for career advancement, arming readers with the knowledge and skills to rise above the competition. They may be delivering incredible results, but without a plan, they risk getting stuck in place. The notion that it's up to the individual to manage their own career is an important realization, but it's just the start. Knowing what steps to take to reach the next level is equally crucial. That's where this guide shines, by providing a clear blueprint for navigating the twists and turns of the professional landscape and ensuring that every ounce of hard work and talent pays off in the form of career growth and fulfillment. It's like an elite training regimen for your career.

—LIEUTENANT COLONEL DONALD M. WIX, Retired US Army, 160th Special Operations Aviation Regiment

Talbot does a great job emphasizing a key point that so many managers fail to understand: it's not about you. It is maddening just how often people assume that large moves involving hundreds of employees were somehow done for the sole purpose of messing them up as individuals. This is but one of many valuable lessons contained in this book and why every aspiring manager should own it.

—JULIUS GAUDIO, hedge fund manager

Talbot Stark has always had a cutting-edge approach that few in the financial markets possess. This book succinctly distills his unique vision. If you're looking for a spark, Elite Performance for Managers will ignite your career. You will master your career and your life with this powerhouse executive playbook.

—COLIN MACINTOSH, founder of the SUND app

For my loving parents, Allen and Natalie Stark;

my wonderful wife, Melissa; my remarkable sons,

William and Luke; and my amazing family and friends

around the world. Without them, my career and this

book would not have been possible.

CONTENTS

A NOTE TO THE READER

"For with God nothing will be impossible."

LK 1:37 NKJV

I am so thankful to God for bringing me into this world and providing me with my loving family. From the moment my father told me that he would not always be there for me, I knew that I had to prepare for the journey ahead. He did his best to help me stand on my own two feet, and it was my mother who was my confidant and the wind beneath my wings. She encouraged me through every stage of my life and career.

Their support and inspiration, as well as that of my wife, sons, other family, and friends, allow me to pay it forward to my readers. They taught me the value of hard work, dedication, and perseverance. They showed me that anything is possible if you believe in yourself and never give up.

With over forty years of experience distilled into a single career guide, my sincere desire is that this book will inspire you to reach for the stars. I hope that it will not only change your career but also change your perspective and your life. I want you to enjoy all the success and happiness you deserve and to help you master you.

I will be with you every step of the way as your coach through my Elite Performance Pillars™, a process of identifying the three areas you need to master with a methodology and specific steps for each that you can start to implement today. This book is meant to change your perspective. It is meant to change your career. It is meant to change your life.

You have the power to achieve greatness. Believe in yourself, stay focused, and never give up on your dreams. Investing in yourself is the best investment you can make. So, start collecting the return on that investment today.

—*Talbot Stark*

Part I

INTRODUCTION

WHY TAKING CHARGE OF YOUR CAREER DEVELOPMENT IS ESSENTIAL IN CORPORATE SETTINGS

"The only person you are destined to become is the person you decide to be."

—RALPH WALDO EMERSON

GONE ARE THE DAYS when a company hired you right out of college, put you through an extensive training program, guided your career through each level, and then gave you a gold watch and a pension upon your retirement. The traditional linear career no longer exists.

As technology and the market change quickly, companies must adapt just as fast to survive. Roles, and sometimes entire departments, are reorganized or eliminated overnight. While some organizations purport to prioritize career management, the reality often falls short. Company leaders are beholden to their shareholders, who are primarily concerned with the company's bottom line, not individual employee growth. Even if you're lucky enough to be assigned to a manager who takes an interest in mentoring you, their primary focus is advancing the organization's interests, as well as their own. They may not have a deep understanding of your aspirations, personal circumstances, or long-term vision. Waiting for them to proactively champion your career goals is like hoping for a lottery win—it's unrealistic. To flourish professionally, you must step up and take ownership of your own career journey.

Additionally, legal considerations further complicate the career development landscape within organizations. Human resources (HR) departments focus on compliance, fair treatment, and safeguarding the company from potential lawsuits. Offering explicit career advice, promises, or guidance can expose the organization to legal risks. Consequently, managers and HR professionals may be reluctant to provide comprehensive coaching.

My passion is to share the life-changing knowledge I have acquired over my lifetime with you in this never-before-written career guide that you can read over a weekend. I do not want anyone else seeking to become an elite performer to miss out on the things they need to know that took me years to acquire and master. This quest inspired me to develop the Elite Performance Pillars™, the origins of which are based on several significant contributors, key lessons from valued mentors and coaches, best practices and techniques I experienced in various settings, my own research, modeling of elite performers, and virtual loop learning (i.e., through trial and error and then refinement). I wrote this book so you have a shortcut and can skip the trial-and-error portion, since I did the experimenting on your behalf and then recorded what works. I want to put you on the fast track.

I often witnessed well-intentioned people, with gifts and capabilities far beyond my own, lose momentum and unintentionally commit career self-sabotage because they were tirelessly working on getting things done but never took the time to manage their careers. They were dutiful and highly capable, the kind of people you want on your team, but no one ever told them that it is not the firm's responsibility, nor your manager's (even if they are the best) to manage your career. It is yours and yours alone.

However, taking time to manage your career and being self-aware alone will not change your career. Time is extremely valuable, so you must use it wisely and avoid falling into the graveyard of stagnated careers. You need to know where to focus and clearly understand the specific steps you need to take to achieve all the success in your career and the joy in your life you deserve. Therefore, I have made it my mission to consolidate these valuable lessons into the career guide I never had—an invaluable elite performance tool kit that allows others to significantly benefit from the trials and tribulations I experienced during the rich tapestry of my life.

The result is a career guide that will offer a compelling return on investment and seventy thousand hours of experience distilled into the three most important facets of one's career, each broken down into ten concise steps to follow. It also applies to any industry, so I guarantee that with the investment of a weekend read and self-application, you can profoundly change your career and your life for the better.

To ensure that you can use this guide in the day-to-day management of your career, I have included short summaries of the key takeaways for each chapter as a ready reference. You can carry it with you, digitize the chapter summaries on your phone, or refer to www.ExecPathfinders.com to obtain the ready reference to the career guide you have been waiting for.

Embrace the fact that your career development rests in your hands and follow the program outlined in this book—it's everything you wish someone would tell you about how to actually manage your career. Should you desire more one-on-one coaching after reading, I'll share even more information about how you can get the support you need to unlock your full potential and create a career path that aligns with your aspirations at the end of the guide. Remember, you are in charge of your career journey and what becomes of it. It's time to get back in the driver's seat.

Congratulations on your commitment to start managing your career today! You will reignite the anxious positive energy that you feel when you are about to start something new and amazing. Kindly make a note to yourself: you are what you repeatedly do, and you are committed to circumventing the career graveyard of the stagnant and the rut of being task-driven and results-focused while never rising above to consciously take your game to the next level.

CHAPTER 1 TAKEAWAYS

- Your company isn't going to manage your career. You must take ownership of your career journey.

- Embrace the fact that your career development rests in your hands.

- Manage your career by following the Elite Performance Pillars™ outlined in this book.

YIN AND YANG

*"Yin and yang are complementary, not opposing forces.
They interact to form a whole greater than themselves."*
—JOHN WOODEN

I GREW UP BELIEVING that an impeccable work ethic would be critical to my long-term success. I thought that, since I worked my way through high school, joined the military, and put myself through university, this applied work ethic would be my key to success. As I progressed in my career, I realized that advancement could be limited if one was, consciously or unconsciously, simply task-focused, just myopically working hard and getting results. Through experience, I learned that perhaps the result in and of itself was not the most important part of advancing in one's career. There is a tipping point in one's management career where the perception of how one achieves the result becomes perhaps equally or more important than the result itself.

Often, the people who are most at risk are those with their noses to the grindstone, applying everything they have to the tasks at hand and remaining steadfastly loyal to the firm. They believe that the best they can do is to accomplish the tasks and objectives that they are given. However, the embedded risk is that their well-intended focus on results can lead to tunnel vision, resulting in an inability to see the big picture. The doer of the task is so focused on the "what" that they forget to focus on the "how." This result-focused mindset concentrates their attention on a particular outcome and filters all information and evidence through the lens provided by that outcome. This can dull their awareness of how they are being perceived and may result in the individual excluding others in the process by concentrating on the accomplishment of the objective.

This is a dangerous path because it can be self-reinforcing. The more they focus on producing results to prove their mettle, the further they distance themselves from colleagues, stakeholders, and senior management.

WHAT IS INTERNALIZED IS EXTERNALIZED

I know how quickly this can turn into a downward spiral because I caught myself midcareer with blinders on, heading rapidly down the path of tunnel vision. Through your tunnel-vision lens, you get things done, close deals, complete projects ahead of time, and add value to the firm. But if you do not quickly correct course by dedicating time to thinking about the *how* and committing time to plan your career, you are at risk. Anxiety builds around you, as people do not have a clear understanding of what your plans are because you are in execution mode, and the self-generated pressure you put on yourself to get more done has the exact opposite effect on the people you work with. Worse, what is internalized is externalized. The more pressure you put on yourself to get things done, the greater the level of internal stress you generate. If you have not carefully planned and brought your boss and colleagues along, they will fear you are taking shortcuts. They will feel uneasy with your pace, and despite your intent to do well, you could be perceived as a risk to the firm.

If you do not quickly change how you perform in the workplace, you will significantly increase the probability that you could be labeled a rogue operator. You may get things done and may even believe that you are doing exactly what management is asking of you, but executing tasks without a keen awareness of how you are perceived can outweigh the very things, "the results," that you are working so hard to accomplish.

Your career is not a Hollywood military movie. The single rogue warrior does not exist on the real-world battlefield, nor does it exist in the corporate world, or at least not for long.

INTELLIGENCE PREPARATION
OF THE CORPORATE BATTLEFIELD

As I discuss later in this book, I served in the US Army. In the military, it is a standard operating procedure that one of the first things you do in preparing for a mission is to conduct an intelligence preparation of the battlefield (IPB). During the IPB, you dedicate critical planning time to studying the battlefield on which you will engage. You study the terrain, the visible obstacles, the hidden obstacles, the potential avenues of approach, and how you would attack or defend this area depending on the scenario.

If you believe that the results will speak for themselves, the critical element you are missing is the need to incorporate the planning process of an IPB. When preparing a mission in the US Army, the IPB was only the first step. We would spend significant time planning how we would coordinate with our friendly units to our left and right flanks. In addition, a comprehensive military operation would entail close coordination with all branches. This would involve meticulous integration and planning for various aspects, such as air support, logistics, artillery, and other combat arms units, as well as support units dedicated to ensuring mission success.

These same requirements exist in the corporate world and are needed to be successful at the elite level. Soft skills absolutely matter. Yes, emotional quotient (EQ) matters, but there is much more to consider. Are you aligned with your boss's objectives today? Things evolve and change. Do not take it for granted that just because something was the top priority at the start of the year that it will remain so. Priorities change, and you must check in to validate. You need to keep your radar up to ensure your present efforts are consistent with the firm's goals and values as they evolve.

So, how do you change your perspective and look out over the corporate landscape/battlefield from the vantage points of colleagues and stakeholders? How do you raise your level of self-awareness such that you are aware of the perception others have of how you achieve the result? Are you bringing everyone along with you? Does your manager and your manager's manager endorse and clearly understand your mission? Or do they see you as a risk?

Has your passion for getting things done been expressed in a fashion that labels you as a rogue? Have you skipped planning steps (or given the impression that you skipped steps) or visible coordination with peers and stakeholders? Perhaps you convinced yourself that the time to market is so important that you do not have time to go through the bureaucracy. Perhaps you think that the rewards for the firm are so significant that your quick actions to achieve the objective are justified.

ONLY YOU CAN MANAGE YOUR CAREER

You think that you have a safety net. You naively think that you don't need to worry about managing your career and instead let the results speak for themselves. You work at an excellent firm, and you have a great manager who you think will help you manage your career. Well, pull out the yellow flag, listen to the downshifting of the engines on the track, slow your speed, and proceed with extreme caution.

Here's the simple truth: It is not the firm's, human capital or resource management's, nor your manager's responsibility to manage your career. It is yours and yours alone. The first misconception is that any firm (including world-class firms) is there to manage your career. The truth is that no firm is aligned with your objectives because each firm has its own objectives. It's not incumbent upon them to outline how you are supposed to manage your career.

This is how I operated: I fed on adrenaline, driving harder, faster, and cornering at greater speeds. If I had been on a track, you would have smelled the rubber adhering to the asphalt as I pushed the car harder, increasing the RPM and intentionally revving into the red zone for the good of the firm. Fortunately, a mentor grabbed me and told me that I was going to blow up. The best Formula 1 drivers do not continually drive their car in the red zone at 7,500 RPM or they would have a very upset sponsor, manager, crew, teammate, or engineering team because the engine would overheat and seize.

ADOPTING YIN AND YANG
INTO YOUR DAILY ROUTINE

My mentor was concerned and told me that I had to incorporate some yin and yang into my day-to-day execution. We both shared an appreciation for martial arts, and he reminded me that they teach you that you can't always be on the attack. You need to give, absorb, and then come back. The secret lies in rocking back and forth, varying your game, taking time to figure out your tactics, observing the situation, planning, and then reacting to it rather than simply executing continuously in the same manner.

MOVING BEYOND TASK EXECUTION

This was my eureka moment. The results themselves are only going to take you so far. Some figure it out through trial and error. At the mid-level point of my career, I found myself in the career abyss. But in this abyss was a bright beam of light. It was the culmination of my military background, experience in martial arts, and a timely revelation pointed out to me by a mentor. If my career was going to advance, I needed to own it. I needed to transform my daily routine from being task-execution-dominant to carving out and prioritizing 5–10 percent of my time to proactively managing the three most important pillars of one's career: (1) Being a Better You (Managing Yourself), (2) Being a Better Manager, and (3) Managing Your Manager.

At this point, you may be following along with what you are reading on these pages, but inherently, there is still pushback. "I'm simply too busy. I have so much on my plate that I don't have the luxury of committing 5–10 percent of my time to managing my career and working with a coach or a mentor. You don't understand. I'm resource-scarce. I'm increasingly being asked to do more with less and simply don't have more time to manage my career."

The good news is that I wrote this career guide specifically for you. It will challenge your old habits and provide a proven three-part system that will enable you to exit the career abyss and transcend not only your career but your personal happiness, and push you into a new upward trajectory. This is a groundbreaking career guide that provides you with the critical career advice that no one else is going to tell you. In addition, I wanted to provide a straightforward, honest approach—a step-by-step guide that you can implement.

I DO NOT HAVE TIME TO MANAGE MY CAREER

Let's address the first objection: I don't have enough time. The first realization is that no one is going to tell you this: work less. Yes, work less. Don't tell your boss that you just purchased a new career guidebook and that you are supposed to work less. That's not my point. My point is for you to not work tirelessly, giving 100 percent at the job only. If you are going to advance in your career, you must commit 5–10 percent of your time to better managing yourself and how you execute your job. I did not realize this until the golden decade of my career, but I do not want you to miss out on one day of implementing this life-changing discipline.

First, if you are going to take on greater responsibilities, you must learn how to delegate and partner efficiently. If you have not built a team that can carry on the mission without you managing or controlling every aspect, you have capped your own career progression (more to come on this when we talk about Pillar II, Being a Better Manager). I will guide you, step by step, to create the time to manage your career, starting today.

Let's assume your work week averages fifty to seventy hours a week, so you need to create somewhere between 1.5–3.5 hours of career planning time. We will discuss this in more detail in Pillar I (Being a Better You), but start by recording how you spend your time in thirty-minute blocks throughout a work week. Find two to three meetings that can be delegated to someone you want to empower on your team. Likewise, find weekly or biweekly meetings you can delegate a representative to attend 50 percent of the time. The most effective way I created time for myself was by taking one to two hours on a Sunday evening, usually after family activities and before dinner (5–7 p.m.). This may

13

not be feasible for everyone, so an alternative is getting up thirty minutes earlier once or twice a week.

UNPLUG TO SPEED AHEAD WITH EFFECTIVENESS

On Sundays, I would spend one to two hours unplugged. No screens, no emails, no TV—just time to myself to think, with a focus on solitude. You'll find that your brain operates incredibly efficiently when you eliminate digital, audial, and visual distractions. Simply shut things off, find a quiet time where you will ideally not be interrupted, and allow your brain power to do a mark to market of where you are. It is truly one secret power that you can unleash for your benefit.

The visualization technique used during this time of solitude is to act as the pilot of your own career, examining the key indicators on the three pillars of your career dashboard. What's important to you? What are you trying to accomplish in your professional life? What are you trying to accomplish in your personal life? Do you take time to reflect on those? If you do, it will significantly help you gain perspective and be increasingly more aware.

My aim is to consolidate the key lessons learned from my life's work, the things from my career that took me years to realize and then internalize, and pass these real career secrets on to you so that you can understand the principles and adapt them in your own way. The heightened mindset I am trying to elicit in this book will allow you to accelerate your career, be more efficient, and be much more aware, or at least have the little internal trigger to step back and admit that you need to accept your situation because something else is happening that you don't understand. It is the realization that there is a required balance, yin and yang, that you must establish to progress.

Success in the workplace isn't just based on what the firm's management tells you or what you execute. You have to create time to proactively manage your career. The ownership of your career and dedicating the required 5–10 percent of your time to managing it are the most important actions you can take. Like anything else, if you don't dedicate time to it, you won't improve or succeed.

In his 2008 book *Outliers*, Malcolm Gladwell wrote that "ten thousand hours is the magic number of greatness."[1] In the book, Gladwell repeatedly mentions the "ten thousand-hour rule," claiming that the key to achieving world-class expertise in any skill is, to a large extent, practicing the correct way for a total of around ten thousand hours. Based on studies in elite performance, Gladwell contended that it's "an extraordinarily consistent answer in an incredible number of fields . . . you need to have practiced, to have apprenticed, for 10,000 hours before you get good."

Gladwell subsequently clarified the often-misunderstood interpretation of the rule: practicing for ten thousand hours alone is not a sufficient condition for success. The point is simply that natural ability requires a huge investment of time to manifest. The simple point for your career is that if you have not previously committed time to manage it, you are already behind.

1   Gladwell, Malcolm. *Outliers*. Penguin UK, 2008.

CHAPTER 2 TAKEAWAYS

- Yin and yang are not opposing forces. They form a whole greater than themselves.

- Tunnel vision focused on results has an embedded risk. Your self-determination and inner drive to produce results can be a detriment because you fail to see the bigger picture.

- Work less to accomplish more. Work, but don't work 100 percent tirelessly at the job. If you are going to advance in your career, you must commit 5–10 percent of your time to better managing your career.

- Gladwell asserts that it takes ten thousand hours to master a skill. The simple point for your career is that if you have not previously committed time to manage it, you are already behind. Start investing the time today to master your career tomorrow.

MY CAREER JOURNEY

"The most difficult thing is the decision to act. The rest is merely tenacity. The fears are paper tigers. You can do anything you decide to do. You can act to change and control your life; and the procedure, the process is its own reward."

—AMELIA EARHART

I GREW UP IN the Midwest with two mentors. The combination of the two most influential people in my life, my father and my uncle, afforded me an amazing journey on which I experienced a great diversity of challenges and roles that defined my career.

My father, a realist, told me, "I will not always be here, my son." I learned to be responsible at an early age with no illusions of a big safety net. This statement fostered an innate tenacity to set my sights on an objective and determine the requirements to successfully move forward.

My other mentor was my uncle, who was an Air Force pilot in Vietnam. He inspired me as he described his travels to exotic places like Thailand and the Philippines. I became obsessed with the flight manuals he would bring home and built a replica of a cockpit under my desk when I was seven. There, I started logging my first hours as a "pilot," visualizing the sky around me as I steadfastly stared at the gauges in my imaginary cockpit and flew to wherever my uncle last visited in the Air Force. My passion for becoming a military pilot was born from my curiosity about my uncle's adventures.

While pursuing an engineering degree at university, I enrolled in the US Army Reserve Officers' Training Corps (ROTC) so I could compete for the opportunity to go to flight school and transition from flying the underside of my desk to flying actual military helicopters. After being commissioned as an officer, completing flight school, training during Desert Shield, and seeing the end of the first Gulf War, I sought my next opportunity in life.

My drive was to find opportunities in international business where I could conduct business affairs with people of diverse nationalities, crisscross the globe at a tenacious pace, and be at the epicenter of change, seeing history unfold in the workplace and participating in the process. When a mentor informed me around the time of the formation of the European Union that Cambridge University was launching a Master of Business Administration (MBA) program, it sounded like an opportunity I could not miss.

After graduating with my MBA, I worked for two dynamic American investment banks in Europe, followed by twenty-plus years at a large global European bank.

My passion for having an international career provided me with an amazing range of experiences, from those in the US military—both domestically and abroad at US Army Europe (USAREUR) headquarters in Heidelberg, Germany—to working at Fortune 500 technology companies and then a career in international finance post-MBA. At times, the leadership roles and expectations of the military contrasted with those of the corporate world. But there was also a common denominator across all of these different contexts since organizations can be quite similar. People gather together and organize themselves in some particular manner to achieve a collective goal or objective. Throughout my diverse career, I saw a common pattern. I frequently observed highly motivated, dedicated, results-oriented people struggle at different points in their careers. Well-intentioned people committed to the firm became so myopic in their tasks, in their zeal to accomplish results, that they did not step back to manage their careers. They did not take time for self-reflection with forward projection.

As I looked in the mirror, I noticed my own reflection. Had I turned into what I had observed for so many years? Highly capable people with proven track records had been caught by this snare trap. Was it my turn now? Was it inevitable that the odds, political machine, and maneuvers would catch up with us if we were a results-oriented professional? Or was there something else completely going on that could explain it?

REINFORCING BAD HABITS ON THE DRIVING RANGE AND IN YOUR CAREER

"With good intent much ill can be done."
—GERMAN PROVERB

I took pride in my work ethic. I was always trying to see how I could push further, make that one extra call, squeeze in one extra meeting to close business, and put more revenue in the bank. I had tunnel vision. I was 100 percent focused on opportunities for the firm. My approach was to be positively tenacious, to use every ounce of energy until exhausted, make no excuses, and leave it all out on the corporate playing field, delivering the result. I was in denial that devoting time to manage my career was a prerequisite for career progression at the elite levels.

Another eureka moment struck me while I was playing golf. My desire to improve my golf game motivated me to visit the driving range and hit a bucket of one hundred balls. I had the best intentions, carefully approaching the ball, setting myself up, and then swinging. But in each of those one hundred swings, I was simply reinforcing my bad habits. I wanted to get better, but was simply executing over and over again. I was willing to put in the work, time, and effort but not to step back and evaluate my swing, contact, and the infinitesimal changes I needed to make to improve. It dawned on me that it was the same as managing one's career.

You have to commit 5–10 percent of your time off the driving range, mastering your art with critical thinking and the key steps that must be followed. Failure to examine how you approach your career can have dire consequences akin to the pro golfer who consistently misses the cut. He has all the mechanics and the raw talent, but somehow, he is not committing 5–10 percent of his time to mental preparation to make the micro changes to his game that will enable him to consistently make the cut and let his innate abilities achieve all the success he deserves.

If you don't manage your career, you will not only fail to succeed but you will burn out and jeopardize your well-being and your personal life, too. The professional and personal costs are high. The consequences of not committing to plan the next stage of your career can impact your job satisfaction, earnings potential, health, personal mindset, stress levels, well-being, relationships, and more. I know because I have been there and want to provide you with a better path forward.

I want to help you make the cut every time in your career. I spent thousands of hours developing and perfecting the Elite Performance Pillars™ (EPP™) methodology to help my private executive coaching clients transform their minds, careers, and destinies. The three pillars are as follows: Pillar I: Being a Better You, Pillar II: Being a Better Manager, and Pillar III: Managing Your Manager.

By reading this book, you too can learn the EPP™ methodology and transform your life. I can assure you a far better return on investment than binge-watching the latest show over the weekend, and you can bypass the many trials and tribulations it took me to develop this methodology. The EPP™ methodology can truly be a game changer when it comes to achieving your professional goals and personal happiness. By following this approach, you can make significant strides in your personal growth and development. So, let's focus on your career and see what you need to do next.

The Elite Performance Pillars™ program I developed made a profound impact on my career and life. It gave me the inner confidence to follow my internal GPS (my unique internal compass) on this amazing journey called my career path. It helped me, as a manager, successfully transition from the old-school method of delegating to partnering with team members and developing missions aligned with their strengths. Perhaps most importantly, I achieved more by working less. The words from one of my first managers echoed in my head: "It is not about how hard you work, it is about how smart you work." I took ownership of how I spent my time and committed 5–10 percent of my time each week to actually managing my career using the three-step process in the Elite Performance Pillars™. The Elite Performance Pillars™ have significantly enhanced my work efficiency and productivity, and they will enable you to do the same.

In the pages ahead, you will learn the untold secrets of mastering your career. Each Elite Performance Pillar™ contains the specific steps you need to take, all conveniently consolidated into this powerful career guide. But this book is not for everyone. It is for those of you who are committed to becoming elite performers. Those who are not all-in can stay on the driving range, continually swinging hard at the ball but never evolving their game, unwilling to step back and watch the video of their swing and apply the tips from their coach to get out of their rut and advance to the next level. But if you are willing to commit to taking control of your career, the transformation will begin today.

The tangible benefits you can enjoy, as my clients have, include the opportunity to accelerate your career by building a better you, leveraging your strengths, and identifying areas for improvement. By following the Elite Performance Pillars™, you'll have an opportunity to develop new skills and competencies that are relevant to your goals and challenges. These skills will help you increase productivity and improve communication, influence, collaboration, and conflict resolution skills. It will also foster trust, respect, and feedback among your team members, enhancing their job satisfaction and work engagement. With the Elite Performance Pillars™, you can align your actions with your desired outcomes, create a positive work culture, enrich your well-being, and improve your resilience, adaptability, and creativity. By following these pillars, you'll be able to balance your work and personal life more effectively.

Hopefully, by this point, you realize that trial and error is not the best approach. Instead, it's essential to plan and implement deliberate actions to ensure the success of your life's work. Your future is far too important to be left to chance or luck. Take control and plan for success to secure a bright and promising career.

If you are willing to step off the career driving range to learn and apply these critical steps to master your life, the Elite Performance Pillars™ will dynamically change your career and your life. The journey ahead will involve not only bold changes but also small subtle changes. The Elite Performance Pillars™ will allow you to truly thrive, see things more clearly, reduce stress, and progress further faster. My passion is to share this game-changing program with you. In the chapters ahead, I will fully equip you with the tools and a proven step-by-step methodology to enable you to successfully navigate the exact path meant for you utilizing your internal GPS.

CHAPTER 3 TAKEAWAYS

- Avoid the trap that many well-intentioned people fall into—fully committed to the firm, myopically focused on their tasks, but too busy to manage their careers.

- You need to commit 5-10 percent of your time to managing your career, which will not only set you on a path to success but allow you to avoid burnout and improve your well-being and personal life, too.

- The journey ahead will involve not only bold changes but also small subtle changes that, if done consistently and continually, will yield significant results and allow you to truly thrive, see things more clearly, reduce stress, and progress further faster.

- The Elite Performance Pillars™ is a methodology that has the power to transform your mind, career, and destiny. The three pillars are as follows: Pillar I: Being a Better You; Pillar II: Being a Better Manager; and Pillar III: Managing Your Manager. Focusing on these critical areas can unlock an individual's potential, leading to greater success in multiple areas of life.

OVERVIEW OF THE EPP™ METHODOLOGY

"It is never too late to be what you might have been."

—GEORGE ELIOT

ARE YOU READY to do what it takes to be an elite professional? You picked up this book because, intuitively, you know you must evolve. There's a voice inside, or maybe just a fear, asking if you're still progressing at the same pace you were ten years ago. What happened to that high-flier euphoria, the runner's high, that feeling that you were knocking down targets systematically?

The firm continues to give you more responsibility. You are amassing momentum. Your area of responsibility continues to increase, and management knows you have a track record of getting things done. However, when you look left, right, and behind, you realize you may no longer be the pacesetter. Your internal voice tells you, "I'm delivering the results. I have my nose to the grindstone, and I anticipate challenges and obstacles. Yet, somehow, I'm missing something. I need to change my perspective. I'm in this career abyss where no one is explicitly telling me what is required of me to move forward."

The bottom line is that on the path to becoming elite, there is a tipping point in one's career where it's no longer simply about achieving and surpassing the result. To make it to the next level, what's equally or perhaps more important than the result is your method, your approach, and the process you use to accomplish the result. You put a lot of effort into achieving these results, but the perceptions you create of how you accomplish the result are of equal or greater importance than the results themselves.

Because you are reading this book, there are a few things I know about you. You have already achieved significant success in your career, yet you are unwilling to rest on your laurels. You picked up this book because you are motivated and driven, as you are seeking out how to up your game and succeed at the elite level.

You are one step ahead of others. You realize that there is a game and that the game has high stakes. But how exactly do you play it? Did you know that if you are going to excel and achieve success at the next level, there are three pillars you must master to be an elite professional? What are these three pillars? What are the rules for each pillar? You are at a critical point: either you master the next moves on the chessboard with precision, or you keep your nose to the grindstone, doing your job but not progressing to the next level or achieving all the success and joy you deserve.

Approaching your life's work with purpose and intention is crucial. Depending solely on trial and error can result in avoidable setbacks and errors. Instead, it is essential to dedicate yourself to planning and strategizing, setting realistic goals, and investing the time to do so. Always remember that your life's undertaking is too valuable to be left to fate.

So, what are the next moves? This book has consolidated multiple decades of experience into a single dynamic three-step process, a.k.a. the Elite Performance Pillars™, that will revolutionize not only your career but your life.

Follow this step-by-step plan and it will take you from the status of achiever to being best in class, an elite performer. But it requires you take action today, with no further delays in implementing the three-step plan to accelerate your career. You need to draw a line in the sand now and ask yourself, "One day or day one?" Decide today and commit to mastering the Elite Performance Pillars™.

Are you ready?

If you said "Yes," let's get started on day one of the EPP™ journey that will change your life.

If you said "No," and you're not willing to commit to changing your life, then put this book down right now. It's written only for those committed to investing their time in managing their careers; growing their personal mastery tool kit; and changing their daily habits in order to significantly change their career, body, mind, source of joy, and inspiration in life.

I'm glad you answered "Yes." Elite professionals are those who know that planning their career is inextricably linked to increasing their level of self-awareness and that taking the time to do so is a critical component of their long-term success and one of the most important uses of their time.

Commit here and now. Make today day one of your journey to becoming an elite performer.

ELITE PERFORMANCE PILLARS™—THE BEST OF THE US ARMY, SILICON VALLEY, AND FINANCE

The Elite Performance Pillars™ are a revolutionary methodology that I have crafted over the course of my extensive career spanning the US military, Fortune 500 technology companies, and leading global financial firms. EPP™ is specifically designed for experienced managers seeking to compete and thrive at the elite levels of their industry. Additionally, EPP™ is a comprehensive guide to mastering the three critical career elements that will form the foundation of your success. From the elite performance morning routine to career management insights, this guide contains everything you need to know to become an elite performer in any field and succeed in any industry. And the best part? No one has ever shared this information with you before—that is, until now.

I was driven to codify the methodology so that you and others seeking to be elite performers could start benefiting immediately from the best career advice I developed over multiple decades. The Elite Performance Pillars™ contain the unique, salient success factors that, once mastered, will make you an elite performer regardless of location, culture, or industry.

Through my extensive experience across various industries and locations, I have discovered that adopting the habits and behaviors of successful individuals is crucial for achieving one's goals. Careful analysis and emulation of these behaviors can help individuals reach their full potential.

I can personally attest to the incredible results of the Elite Performance Pillars™ methodology. As a practitioner, mentor, and executive coach, I have seen firsthand how this approach can completely transform careers and lives. The techniques are based on proven breakthrough career management strategies that consistently deliver game-changing outcomes. I highly recommend the Elite Performance Pillars™ to anyone looking to achieve their professional goals and reach new heights of success. The EPP™ are uniquely designed for highly motivated managers seeking to be elite performers. It represents the consolidation of seventy thousand hours of life experience into a single three-step career guide.

I designed the EPP™ specifically for managers, as we are the leaders in the workplace. As managers, it is our responsibility to provide clarity to the team regarding the goals and objectives we seek to accomplish together. Much can be lost if the message is unclear—not only in the proficiency of the team but in your effectiveness as a leader. How many times have you heard "What do they (management) want now?" or "I don't understand what they want us to do" after attending a management meeting?

Yes, it can happen to all of us. Sometimes, the very comments above may be said about your town hall or quarter-end update. As elite performers, you must hold yourself to a higher standard. When the stakes are highest and your clarity of communication has real life-and-death impact, your craft is honed to perfection. Thus, for effective management communication, I incorporated the battle-tested leadership and management techniques from the US Army, specifically the Aviation and Infantry combat arms branches, as well as my years of service in one of the highest military headquarters outside the United States, the US Army Europe Headquarters in Heidelberg, Germany.

Technology shapes everything we do. The advent of artificial intelligence (AI) and other advancements will impact the workplace significantly. How can you stay nimble in the technology industry when things evolve quickly? The Elite Performance Pillars™ further evolved through the valuable experience I gained by capturing the key takeaways from the contributions of elite performers of Silicon Valley, including early leaders of supercomputers like Amdahl; pioneers of Silicon Valley like Hewlett-Packard; and one of the first developers of AI, IBM (with Watson). Technology continues to evolve, but how one successfully adapts to each technological paradigm shift is based on several key principles incorporated into the EPP™ that you can consistently apply to ensure you adapt and stay nimble in your career.

For the last twenty-five-plus years of my career, I worked in London across a diverse range of global roles for both leading US and European banks. This dynamic, international, fast-paced industry was where I discovered that there was a common denominator throughout. Elite professionals consistently mastered the three areas detailed in the Elite Performance Pillars™ in their organization. This was where I crystallized the underpinning methodology and the three critical pillars one must master to be an elite performer.

I hope that the excitement I have to share the Elite Performance Pillars™ with you almost jumps off this page because it is the culmination of my lifelong journey, a quest to successfully research, develop, and model a step-by-step guide to being an elite performer. I have successfully tested, honed, and implemented the Elite Performance Pillars™ as they have continued to evolve over the years with each of their successful deployments across a variety of environments.

Together, let's delve into these performance pillars and unlock your true potential! The Elite Performance Pillars™ consist of the three imperative elements that all elite performers master. It starts with (1) Being a Better You (mastering you), which enables you to start (2) Being a Better Manager, and in turn, you can accelerate your career advancement by (3) Managing Your Manager.

Investing the time to be a better you enables you to be a better manager. We will identify the specific steps you need to take to be an elite manager. Finally, you will learn how to manage your manager. This process is often mishandled because the critical aspect is to see yourself from your manager's perspective—that is, to see the other as the other sees oneself. These steps are not available in any corporate manual, and rarely will a manager provide them to you directly, which is why I specifically developed a methodology based on the most successful techniques for managing your manager that I witnessed over my career.

Each of the pillars that make up the Elite Performance Pillars™ was developed in a real-world context, bringing you the best methods utilized by elite performers across a wide range of industries and coupled with my own research of the steps required to master each of these pillars. The true power of this method is that the core tenets and principles of the Elite Performance Pillars™ enable one to be an elite performer universally. The Elite Performance Pillars™ are sector-independent. The clients I work with find the process equally effective whether their careers are in technology, finance, or health care and no matter the organizational size or culture. The same step-by-step methodology has proven successful in a large domestic firm, a leading multinational firm headquartered in Europe, and a small software firm located on the East Coast of the US; the common denominator throughout is people.

As you begin your journey, rest assured that the Elite Performance Pillars™ will serve as an invaluable investment in your personal tool kit. By mastering these pillars through professional development, you'll be equipped to excel in any environment. Trust in yourself and your abilities and success will surely follow.

THE JOURNEY AHEAD

My mission is to share this career-changing methodology with you so you can reap the benefits, as I have in my own career. It has enabled me to trust in myself, successfully apply the Right Angle Rule of self-development (being true to yourself—find out more in Chapter 5), and commit 100 percent to my next career destination as determined by my internal GPS (also find out more in Chapter 5).

As a senior manager, I witnessed the career-accelerating results of the Elite Performance Pillars™ in the people that

I mentored over the decades that enabled them to success-fully navigate complex organizations and become elite per-formers by locking in on the three key pillars and fully ap-plying the techniques to managing their careers. Recently, I have been fortunate enough to witness firsthand the power of the Elite Performance Pillars™ while coaching executives from all corners of the globe. It has been incredibly reward-ing to see the many benefits my clients have experienced as a result of implementing these pillars, such as strength-ening their relationships with their management team and incorporating the elite performance morning routine into their daily routines. By taking ownership of their mornings, they have gained significant advantages both physically and mentally, allowing them to tackle each day with renewed vigor and purpose.

A NOTE TO THE READER: To help tailor the Elite Performance Pillars™ specifically to you and make this program as successful as possible, I have created an Elite Performance Pillars™ self-assess-ment, which can be found at *www.execpathfinders. com/assessment*. Please take a few minutes now to access the website and complete the Elite Perfor-mance Pillars™ self-assessment.

Congratulations! You are already exercising lead-ership and taking your first step toward becoming an elite performer! Welcome! I am thrilled to have you on board with me and the rest of my clients and readers! Together, we can work toward accelerating your career and achieving all the happiness and suc-cess you deserve. Let's get started.

After taking the assessment, you will receive an email with feedback on the outcomes that highlight areas where you should be focusing your energy to master the Elite Performance Pillars™. This should help you discover how you can become an elite performer by doing what the other 95 percent are unwilling to do. I kindly encourage you to take the assessment now at the start of the program and again at the end of the book to note your progress and areas for future development. Now, back to the book.

WHEN I THOUGHT ONLY RESULTS MATTERED: BEFORE THE ELITE PERFORMANCE PILLARS™

Unlike you, no one told me that the path to becoming an elite performer required mastery of the Elite Performance Pillars™. In the early part of my career, I was not aware of the entirety of the Elite Performance Pillars™. My mindset was singularly focused on the sole idea that becoming an elite performer required an impeccable work ethic and a track record of not just achieving the objective but significantly surpassing the objective. My belief system was as follows: "I will be judged on my results and as an elite performer. I will consistently deliver results that either meet or surpass the objective and do so on time or ahead of schedule, every time." This served me well in the early part of my career, but as I progressed up the management ranks, something changed.

I am sure some of you can relate. In the initial five to ten years post-university, you are on the fast track, exceeding expectations, making promotions ahead of schedule, and entering the early stages of your management career. Then, somehow, the rules change. The management ranks are crowded and the requirements for the next rung up the ladder are less intuitive and not simply based on results. So, what are the rules?

Throughout my career, I've had the opportunity to participate in a multitude of career and leadership development programs. I was fortunate to have managers who were thoughtful and would carefully outline the goals for the year ahead and provide constructive feedback during my appraisals. I would be dutiful and create a visual representation of my top three to five objectives (as I still do today). This helped me stay focused and motivated throughout the year. I believed that as long as I accomplished these objectives, I could continue to advance in my career.

I'd go back to the grindstone, myopically focused on producing the results that were expected of me, ready to commit even more energy and tenacity to the task at hand in my sincere attempt to become an elite performer. I really wish someone would have told me that it is not what you achieve but how you achieve it. I wish someone would have told me that just focusing on delivering results is only a part of career progression, and if you are too focused on just those results, it can be detrimental to your career. That's because in your attempt to do more, you can be seen as a rogue operator, and others may not follow your approach or may view you as self-serving. That is why it is absolutely necessary to step back and gain perspective.

Moreover, I wish someone would have told me that if I truly aspired to be an elite performer, I would need to master Being a Better You—the first pillar of the Elite Performance Pillars™. But this is only one of three pillars you must accomplish if you are going to enter the arena of elite performers.

As I felt my career plateau, I firmly believed, "Let the results speak for themselves." As a matter of fact, I thought my competitive advantage was that I could outwork the next person, increase my focus, utilize my results-driven mindset, double down, and do even more.

If you believe this as I did, but want to become an elite performer, then this book is written for you. Yes, to become an elite performer, you must be driven and motivated. A top performer seeking to ascend to elite status must be hungry for success and fulfillment and ready to put in the work. You must also have self-confidence and be ready to cultivate excellence. However, the part that few, if any, career development programs will teach you is that having a proven track record of delivering results in and of itself is not enough to propel you to the elite level.

Do you believe that results are not enough? Are you willing to step back and challenge yourself? Will the results alone set you up to progress and take on more responsibility? You may be thinking, "I always deliver, exceed my budgets, and consistently complete my projects ahead of time. Weekends are an extension of my workweek. I am all in, dedicated to my work, and not someone who believes in excuses. I deliver, no matter how high the bar, and regularly work twelve-hour days, and the results speak for themselves."

This is your wake-up call. You have successfully reached your ceiling if this is your mantra. To make it to the next level, it is not just about the *what* (results you have delivered) but *how* you accomplished the result. So, let's dive into Elite Performance Pillar™ I: Being a Better You.

CHAPTER 4 TAKEAWAYS

- The Elite Performance Pillars™ apply to any firm or corporate setting.

- By mastering these pillars through professional development, you will be equipped to excel in any environment. Trust in yourself and your abilities, and success will surely follow.

- Results (the what you achieve) are not enough to propel you to the elite level. How you achieve results matters greatly.

PART II

PILLAR I:
BEING A
BETTER YOU

COMMIT TIME TO EVOLVE

"What's dangerous is not to evolve."
—JEFF BEZOS

BEING A BETTER you requires you to understand the how, which entails increasing your level of self-awareness. To gain self-awareness, you must step back and focus on the perceptions people have of how you accomplish the task. Are you inclusive? Do both your N+1s (people you report to) and N-1s (people who report to you) have a clear understanding of the steps you plan to take to accomplish the result? How do you inform other stakeholders regarding your intended process, and do you provide them with an opportunity to offer feedback?

To do all these things, to reflect on your *how*, requires time—not just time on tasks, but time on planning your communications, on the involvement of others, and on the perception you create of being open to feedback. The first thing I will tell you is that you must invest in yourself if you are to become an elite performer.

To evolve beyond a "the results will speak for themselves" mentality, you must commit time to managing your career. At minimum, you need to commit 5–10 percent of your weekly work hours to managing your career. You may be thinking, "I'm already too busy. The one thing I need is more time." I'll tell you, "You need to start doing less to accomplish more."

In hindsight, keeping busy with tasks was my crutch. It made me feel good. It was rewarding: plan, execute, and repeat. However, I had to break this pattern of being busy (tactical) but not taking time to manage my career (strategic). It actually takes a great deal of courage to step away from the production line that can feed your endorphins with the short-term pleasure of results to book time in your calendar to be strategic and manage your career.

TIME IS THE COMMON DENOMINATOR

The most valuable asset anyone has is time. No matter how much money you have, no matter where you sit in the corporate structure, and no matter how old or young you may be, you cannot buy more of it. Everyone has the same amount of time. It is finite—twenty-four hours each day. So, the differences in individual outcomes and performance are a result of how each of us uses our time each day. Elite performers know this.

Ask yourself, do you think your boss or your boss's boss has more responsibilities than you have? More demands on their time? More meetings? More emails? If your aspired destination is to take it all the way to the top, then it is critical that you start changing how you spend your time and start investing 5–10 percent of your time in managing your career today.

Anything worthy of your time requires a plan to execute. Failing to plan is planning to fail, and this adage also applies to your career. When I ask prospective clients in my executive coaching business if they spend at least thirty to sixty minutes a week managing their career, sadly, many answer "No." This is quickly followed up by, "I know I should, but I don't. I get too busy, too distracted," or "I plan to, but end up dealing with problems instead. Crisis issues crowd out the time I intend to dedicate to managing my career."

Notice that I said many executives answer "No," but not all. Elite professionals know that planning their careers and increasing their levels of self-awareness, and making time for both, are critical components of their long-term success and two of the most important uses of their time.

Before taking on a new client at ExecPathfinders, my executive coaching company, I ask them to commit to meeting for either thirty minutes a week or one hour every two weeks for six months as a condition of our engagement. Some potential clients are not able to make this commitment, but for their good and welfare, I pass on the following advice: "If you're not willing to invest thirty minutes a week in managing your career, how successful do you think you'll be in managing your career overall?" The truth is that there are no shortcuts to success in life. If you're not willing to put in the effort, your career growth will likely plateau.

The first pillar in the EPP™ is creating a better version of yourself and dedicating time to managing yourself and your career. At the executive and senior management levels, it's a finesse game. It's the dedication to small, incremental, almost infinitesimal changes sustained continuously that can yield significant results. It's a mindset of committing yourself to excellence and upholding the belief that excellence is accomplished methodically. This is where an executive coach can really help you identify the specific areas where small changes can have large positive payoffs in terms of your career advancement and development. My most satisfying results come from working with clients who have the willpower and discipline to master the Elite Performance Pillars™. I can accelerate the process by identifying the specific areas to develop that can be blind spots but which an executive coach like me can spot more readily.

Perhaps the most noteworthy recent example of how small changes can have a big impact can be found in the sporting world. According to the concept of marginal gains, if you improve every aspect of your performance by 1 percent, you will achieve a significant increase when you put them all together. This strategy was used from 2003–2008 by the British Cycling organization, which went from mediocre to dominant in just five years by making small improvements to everything from bike seats to hand washing.

Elite performers adopt the same mindset of complete dedication to small daily improvements and positive changes in their habits that can yield life-changing results. The focus is twofold: (1) increasing one's awareness to improve their self-mastery and (2) helping develop the professional capabilities required for the path ahead.

We are building a foundation for your career using a systematic approach, and this first step is to build the best you. It requires paying attention to the details, just as a coach works with the world's best golfers by observing their swing and making minute adjustments to take them from being a professional to being an elite professional who consistently makes the cut. This discipline requires gaining an understanding of your strengths, owning your weaknesses, and making a commitment to continuously make incremental progress to yield significant results. Additionally, it requires you to evolve your focus from not just achieving results but to paying careful attention to *how* you accomplish the results.

In the next chapters, we will identify the other specific steps you need to take to develop your professional pedigree, enabling you to succeed at the next level.

The critical success factors include raising your awareness; changing your perspective; and committing to making the changes in your communication, attitude, and day-to-day interactions with your manager that often get overlooked or misunderstood but have an impact far beyond just delivering on your objectives. It is the understanding of the processes involved in *how* you achieve the result that will hone your skills and mindset to improve your awareness so you can execute consistently with excellence.

MANAGING YOU

Starting with the end in mind and setting clear goals for oneself is crucial to determining one's destiny. It's a process that requires introspection and self-reflection, because the first step to shaping your future lies within you. One needs to harken back to what drove their ambitions when they were a child. Revisit those moments when life was less complicated. When I was young, life was so much simpler, and my imagination knew no bounds. I can still feel the excitement of soaring through the clouds and embarking on thrilling adventures as I flew my imaginary plane, staring at my hand-drawn instrument panel while sitting under my desk.

This love for flying stirred my passion and inspired me to pursue my first career goal of becoming a military pilot, which was where my internal GPS took me in the first phase of my life journey. However, my fascination with global travel and business soon took center stage and became my new driving force. It was this passion that led me down the path of finance, and I am grateful for where it has taken me.

When reflecting on the past, it's essential to hold on to the things that ignited our childhood inspiration and use them as a catalyst to pursue our aspirations. Take a moment to pause and reflect. What activities or experiences bring happiness and peace of mind to you? Where do you get lost in your head, drift off, and disconnect from the physical things around you? Your mind is in control, and it's driven by your internal compass. That inner voice that aligns your will, your dream, your passion, and your curiosity can take you wherever you want to go.

During my childhood, my uncle—who was twenty years my senior—was my hero, my mentor. He was an Air Force C-141 pilot in Vietnam, and his bravery and dedication to our country inspired me greatly. As he transitioned from being a military pilot to commercial flying, he gave me a gift that I treasured throughout my formative years. My uncle gave me the pilot's manual for a Boeing 727, and I couldn't believe what I saw when I opened it up. On the first few pages was a poster of a full mock-up of the instrument panel. It was like I had been given a sneak preview into the future. Suddenly, I could see myself as the pilot of this incredible aircraft, soaring through the sky and experiencing the thrill of flight like never before. It was an exhilarating feeling that I will never forget. I am forever grateful for his guidance and support, which have left a lasting impact on my life.

FLY YOUR DREAM

From my earliest childhood memories, I can recall carefully trying to replicate the instrument panel from my uncle's flight manual on the underside of the desk that my father made me. I used markers to draw the altimeter that displayed aircraft altitude, the magnetic direction indicator (a type of compass), an artificial horizon, and the vertical airspeed indicator. Sitting on the floor looking up at the underside of my desk was my cockpit—the cockpit of my life. I visualized what it would be like to fly—to be the pilot of my plane. It was my passion, my dream, and the driver of my life.

I think, deep down, we all have that one thing that we are meant to do. It's the thing that makes our hearts race, the thing that puts smiles on our faces, and the thing that fills us with excitement and a little bit of fear. It's like when riding a rollercoaster and you are at the top of the climb, you know that the drop is coming, but for just a moment, you're suspended in mid-air, feeling alive and wondering what's next. For that moment, you are almost motionless, somewhat fearful of what lies ahead but, at the same time, exhilarated and intrigued by who the future you will be.

THINGS YOU CAN DO VERSUS THINGS THAT YOU WANT TO DO

This impassioned feeling is simply the physical and mental alignment of where you want to be—the future projection of you. Innately, you know what you want to do, where your passions lie, and are cognizant of the God-given talents that lie within. Here is one of my first truisms: in life, there are things you *can* do and then there are things that you *want* to do.

This point is so important: there is a difference between what you can do and what you want to do. As an engineering student at the University of Wisconsin–Madison, my dream job was to work for IBM. I secured a co-op position at IBM and headed out to Binghamton, New York. This was in the very early days of CAD/CAM design, in which the job entailed sitting in dark rooms and using the tools at the time to design the required layouts for production lines within the factory. I lived the truism—I *could* spend my day staring at my screen in almost complete solitude to design a new production line, but it was complete torture for me. There was no interaction with team members, no buzz of preparing a presentation, no techniques utilized to respond to an RFP (request for proposal). Instead, there was the hypnotizing task of designing something on a computer screen with the rudimentary tools available at the time. I quickly learned there was a big difference between the things I *could* do as an engineering student and the things I *wanted* to do. CAD/CAM design was something within my repertoire of capabilities but definitely not something that I wanted to do, nor did it leverage my innate people skills. Rather, it was limited to the academic discipline I studied.

But here is the trick. If you are true to yourself, really focus, and believe and trust your internal GPS, it will set the path for the journey ahead. That path will test you on things you have to do, but all of these are requirements for you to achieve your goal of what you want *to be* and, ultimately, what you want *to do*. However, to push yourself through the things that you may find mundane, difficult, and unnecessary will require your intestinal fortitude: a military term I like to use.

For me, and I am sure for many of you, life will not be one destination but rather a series of different careers, roles, and challenges that your inner compass will point to. This is the joy of life—the unlimited opportunities and adventures you can seek out and experience. I want to share with you the journey I have enjoyed and, most importantly, the lessons and key principles I learned along the way so that you can apply these at any stage of your journey. We start with the most important pillar of the career guide: Being a Better You.

YOUR INTERNAL GPS

We all come from different pasts, blessings, challenges, and upbringings, but we share one common denominator: we all must stay true to ourselves. I do not know you yet. We have not met, but I know a few things about you. I can sense that you are on a mission to better yourself. You want to compete at the highest level, and you have a deep passion and drive to succeed. That is why you are here, seeking guidance on how to effectively manage your career. You recognize that your career is one of the most important aspects of your life, which is why you've picked up this book and are willing to put in the work to improve yourself and invest your valuable time in adding precious tools to your personal tool kit.

My hope is that each of you will tap into that inner child under the desk and discover what truly makes you happy. You know it; it resides inside of you. That inner voice within you is your internal GPS, guiding you toward your true purpose. Your personality, aspirations, physical attributes, and mental gifts all come together to make you uniquely you. Trust yourself, and never lose sight of who you are.

You must remove any barriers from your environment, including what parents, friends, teachers, and others may have told you. Do not take a self-limiting outlook on possibilities. Instead, focus on the contrary. Remove any voices and any predispositions. The world is your canvas. How do you want to use the unique talents that define you? Suppress the voices that say you should choose this career because that's what your father or mother did, or that it's the best path for a lucrative career, or that you could never do that, or that your talents are wasted doing that.

Instead, trust your internal GPS. Remove the limitations. Open up your field of vision and set sail to that destination for your career. Step outside the small circle of what is possible and step into the unconstrained world of possibilities. Take some time to be by yourself. Whether it's taking a leisurely walk, going on a run, or just sitting and enjoying the world around you, it's important to take a break from the hustle and bustle of everyday life. When you're alone, listen to your internal GPS. It's more than just a voice—it's a built-in guidance system that can help you navigate through life. Remember to be brave enough to do the things you *can* do so you can accomplish the things you truly *want* to do. Trust your instincts and don't be afraid to pursue your dreams with boldness and determination.

Don't drive your career looking in the rearview mirror. There is no future in the past. Do not let disappointments, failings, or negative memories of the past in any way shape the potential of your future—there is no correlation. The career journey ahead will be correlated to the path of least resistance for you. This is the zone where things feel effortless to you; you thrive on it, enjoy it, and are in your zone. This inner confidence is why your internal GPS is so powerful.

Based on your unique capabilities, desires, and sources of joy in life, you will discover where you can not only excel but find joy in doing what you do. You have the potential to shine the most when you do what you love. Keep pushing yourself and never lose sight of the passion that drives you forward—this is your internal GPS. You have the ability to excel beyond measure. This is the path that you must follow, and your internal GPS will guide you if you let it. Tapping into this powerful internal guidance system is the secret to realizing your true potential. It is out there on the horizon, far beyond the curvature of the Earth. Trust it, and it will take you there.

On your journey, realize that the destinations may change, like a passenger who may have some connections along the way to their final destination. Stay steadfast and pursue the path of least resistance for you as determined by your internal GPS. Trust your internal GPS. Remove any limitations and set sail to your next career destination. Find the aspects, challenges, and roles that bring you joy and drive your passion. George Bernard Shaw described this self-actualization as "Being used for a purpose recognized by yourself."[2]

---

2   Shaw, George Bernard. *Man and Superman*. Penguin, 1903.

THE RIGHT ANGLE RULE

The concept of a right angle is well defined in geometry, where it is an angle that measures exactly 90 degrees. However, in the realm of self-development, the Right Angle Rule takes on a whole new meaning. It involves recognizing both your self-image, the person you see in the mirror (horizontal leg), and God's knowledge of the truth (the vertical leg) to form the true you. This intersection (the true you) forms a 90-degree or right angle and is the basis of the rule. Embracing this rule can help individuals gain a deeper understanding of themselves and their place in the world.

Acknowledging one's true feelings, thoughts, and beliefs, even if they are uncomfortable or difficult to accept, is a crucial aspect of self-reflection and introspection. However, it is not always easy to be honest with oneself. Many people rationalize their behavior and reassure themselves with self-talk that is more wishful thinking than actual truth. Research studies at UCLA and MIT have found that a simple reminder to be honest with oneself works most of the time.[3] This is where the Right Angle Rule comes into play. By embracing this rule as a reminder to stay honest, elite performers can train themselves to be more truthful and authentic in their self-reflection and interactions with others.

Being honest with oneself has many benefits, including improved self-awareness, increased self-confidence, better decision-making, higher-quality relationships, and reduced stress.[4] Earlier in this chapter, I shared with you my personal experience as a co-op student at IBM. The Right Angle Rule helped me recognize my strengths and weaknesses

3   Suzanne Kane, "How to Be Honest With Yourself," Psych Central, last modified August 19, 2017, https://psychcentral.com/blog/how-to-be-honest-with-yourself.

4   Christopher D. Connors, "Honesty—How it Benefits You and Others," Medium, September 7, 2016, https://medium.com/the-mission/honesty-how-it-benefits-you-and-others-ecb3e7fabb9a.

and understand my true passions and desires. It made me realize that I was not cut out for CAD/CAM design despite having the qualifications for the position. As Pillar I of the EPP™ is about creating a better version of yourself, I firmly believe that embracing the Right Angle Rule can help elite performers gain a greater sense of purpose and achieve their full potential.

I live by the Right Angle Rule, which means being honest with myself and God. There is no room for cheating or taking shortcuts since the man in the mirror and the man above always know the truth. Use the Right Angle Rule and be true to yourself when visualizing your career destination. Align your passions, skills, and motivations to achieve true joy and ultimate happiness.

This rule is a good thing in that if you truly let go, you will revert to the mean, come back to center, and be true to yourself. Your internal GPS will guide you toward your destinations, and along the way, you will have to do things to prove that you can reach them, but these are simply steps along the path to your chosen destination.

I studied engineering to follow in my uncle's footsteps. I understood this to be a good major for a career and to be a military pilot. I was strong in math, and I saw engineering as something I could do. These stepping-stones provided a strong foundation that enabled me to do what I *wanted* to do but were also requirements that allowed me to follow my internal GPS.

PILLAR I: BEING A BETTER YOU

Building the first pillar of the Elite Performance Pillars™ is about managing you. The fact is, no one cares more about you than you. Simply put, be diligent in whatever you do, be exhaustive, and research everything yourself. Be respectful of others and seek advice, but ultimately, you must know this: it is yours to own. This is both empowering as well as daunting.

Following your internal GPS is not putting your feet up on the dashboard. It is an athletic stance in which you are balanced on the balls of your feet, ready to pivot left or right to fully explore your options. As a kid growing up in the Midwest, my internal GPS set a destination, but it was up to me to navigate the path and connect the dots to pursue my dream of becoming a military pilot.

University was a self-funded endeavor. In high school, I began to explore all the options. I looked at the military academies first, but their engineering programs were five-year degrees plus a seven-year commitment as a pilot. At the age of sixteen, the thought of committing five years plus another seven years felt like I was going to be as old as my uncle by the time I completed my obligations. Guidance counselors knew the basics, but had not done the due diligence to explore all the options of each branch of service or the various options within each branch to become a commissioned officer and pilot.

The Army had unique programs: the Early Commissioning Program (ECP) and the Simultaneous Membership Program (SMP). To participate, you had to take several cognitive and personality tests and then apply in the first semester of twelfth grade. The program required you to join the US Army Reserve in high school and attend active duty basic training during the summer of your senior year. If you successfully graduated, you would join the Army ROTC program as a junior during your freshmen year of college. Throughout the school year, you would participate in ROTC and spend one weekend per month doing US Army Reserve training.

This program was a fast track since you could become a

commissioned officer at the end of your sophomore year of university and then enter a six-year reserve officer commitment, which included the active duty Officer Basic Course, flight school, and your reserve training. The program paid you as an E-5 (enlisted rank of sergeant) when you were a cadet performing US Army Reserve weekend drills. My internal GPS filed the flight plan for my first career destination of becoming an engineer—something I could do—in order to do something I wanted to do, which was become a military officer and pilot.

This is the mindset that you must embrace. Clear any mental limitations from your mind—all the voices that said do this or do not waste your time doing that. It is like removing metal objects away from the perimeter of an old-school compass. The same goes for your internal GPS—remove any objects that could prevent the compass's needle from pointing to true north.

When I silenced all the past voices and removed any ideas that could interfere with my internal GPS, I had several thoughts about the next phase of my career, following my initial aim of flying in the military.

My internal GPS took me on an amazing journey from a five-year-old boy flying a desk to becoming a military officer at nineteen and a pilot at twenty-five years old. This was just the first destination in my career journey.

CAMBRIDGE UNIVERSITY: THE NEXT DESTINATION

After returning from military duty in Germany, a mentor told me that the University of Cambridge in England was launching an MBA program. The interviews were in-person, so I went to Cambridge to be considered. I was keenly aware that the European Union was due to be launched in 1992, just a few years shy of fifty years after World War II. It was an exciting time of unparalleled opportunity to be there at the start of this amazingly ambitious project to unify the economic interests of the member states. My internal GPS was locked onto the next destination in my life journey.

I always enjoyed the chance to interact with people from diverse nationalities and backgrounds while partaking in the modus operandi, which was the underlying current of getting things done in a commercial setting. I found the fast-paced, high-energy environment of global business to be incredibly invigorating, and I appreciated the opportunity to use my skills and passion for people to achieve our objectives and conclude deals together with a win-win mindset.

I desired to travel with a purpose so I could conduct business globally and enjoy the challenge of dealing with different backgrounds, nationalities, languages, and upbringings that brought me so much satisfaction. The common factor throughout was that I would be dealing with people. Several months later, I received the good news that I had been accepted into the Cambridge MBA program. However, there was bad news—it was very expensive, and it was not obvious how I could get someone to sponsor me since I simply didn't have the means to fund the expenditure myself.

Trust me, in 1992, shortly after the first Gulf War, this was no small feat. The economy was soft. I didn't have the $100,000 tuition for an MBA. However, I did have a fax machine and one of those early word processing typewriters. My internal GPS was locked in, and now I was doing everything that I *could* do to do what I *wanted* to do—attend Cambridge University.

After months of tirelessly sending faxes; making expensive phone calls; and reaching out to countless consulting firms, financial institutions, and global Fortune 500 companies, I finally managed to secure a hybrid sponsorship from a leading technology firm Hewlett-Packard (HP). I attended Cambridge Judge Business School for my MBA, paid for by the sponsor, and when school was not in session, I applied what I learned in academia in the workplace at HP. Securing the sponsorship was a long and arduous process, but I never gave up on my dream and remained persistent in my efforts until I achieved my goal.

I share this with you because you have the same internal GPS within you. Find the aspects that bring you joy, that drive your passion and energy, and let your internal GPS determine the next destination in your career path. Use the Right Angle Rule that requires you to be completely honest with the person in the mirror. God above is the referee to keep you honest, because He knows the truth. Be true to yourself when visualizing the aspects and characteristics of the destination of your career and your life—those that play to your strengths. Silence the noise, advice, and biases of the past, and be honest with yourself. Enthusiastically take note of the characteristics that you want in your job and combine them with what you passionately enjoy doing.

TAP INTO YOUR INFINITE POTENTIAL

Right now presents a unique opportunity to really explore your infinite potential, to achieve your true joy and ultimate happiness by aligning your passions and motivations with your innate strengths. Then, make the conscious commitment to seek out this role so that you can enthusiastically put all of you to work every day, tapping into the things that you excel at and that come naturally to you.

To let your internal GPS truly choose the destination, you need to understand how your brain works. There are two processes that power your internal GPS. The first is not to be rigid and analytical in thought but to instead trust your innate senses. Describe how you feel facing the challenge of coding in a new high-level language, designing that aerodynamic wing, or interacting with people to conduct commerce. Focus on the description of the activities, not what's prescribed. The second is that it's important to always listen to your internal GPS, whether you're relaxing on the sofa or taking a long walk outside. Finding a comfortable spot to escape and listen to music or dream can help you tune out distractions and focus on your inner voice. Trust your instincts and follow the path that feels right to you.

Rely on your intuition rather than a reasoned list of pros and cons and trust your insights rather than data. Let go of the controls. Your internal gyroscope will self-level the plane and your internal GPS will guide you toward your next destination. Stay on your flight path until flying this leg of your career is fun and enjoyable and it feels like autopilot.

When you follow your internal GPS, it's important to remember that you won't always be on a straight path. Just like a pilot makes adjustments to stay on course, you'll need to make small corrections along the way. But as long as you keep your destination in mind and have a clear idea of where you're headed, you'll get there eventually. Don't get discouraged by minor setbacks or detours, just keep adjusting your course and you will reach your goal. Also, be passionate in your career and stay focused on the vision that drives and compels you each day.

You are now in the process of determining your next career destination. You know that you will get there, much like a pilot continually making adjustments along the way. Most importantly, like any commercial pilot, you must trust your instruments, which in your case is your internal GPS.

As you embark on your journey, your instinct and drive are more important than any degrees or credentials you may have. While your skills and education are valuable assets, they can always be refined and improved. Do not worry too much about having all the right skills or qualifications, as these things can always be learned and adapted as you go. Your path may not always be clear, but trust in your own abilities and take action toward your passions. Don't let doubt or fear hold you back. Trust in yourself and push forward toward your goals. Keep moving forward with confidence and determination and rely on your internal GPS, and you will find success in whatever you choose to pursue.

Remember that your intuition and determination will ultimately lead you to success. Along the way, you'll find your path. However, be prepared for bumps in the road. Some may necessitate that you buckle up. When the flight hits turbulence, know this: your resolve and ability to internalize your focus will get you through the storm.

Your internal GPS knows where you're heading. Your path may change, but you know that you began the journey with the end in mind. One powerful tool that many successful people use is the practice of visualization to help them see their goal.

THE POWER OF VISUALIZATION

Accomplished athletes think, see, and role-play every step in their minds. The high jumper visualizes arching their back as each vertebra clears the bar. The quarterback visualizes the ball leaving their hand, starting the rotation that creates a perfect spiral. The free-climber maps out in their mind thousands of different grabs, foot placements, and fingerholds as they ascend the face of a cliff.

I truly believe in the power of visualization. Focusing on a goal and visualizing accomplishing it has been the fuel and motivation that has driven me in my career. It has allowed me to transcend the confines of my Midwest origins and accompany my uncle on his remarkable journeys by envisioning myself charting a similar path in the years ahead. When individuals visualize themselves performing a task successfully, their brain responds as if they're actually performing the task. This mental rehearsal can lead to improved performance and increased confidence. The power of visualization lies in its ability to engage the mind and body, creating a powerful feedback loop that can be used to achieve a wide range of goals.

Visualization is the first step of realization. What do you visualize? What picture is in your mind when you wake up in the morning? Let your mind be free. Don't worry about the job or how to get there. Simply think about what excites you, what drives you, what intrigues you. Let that be your target, the visualized state that you pursue.

Many people are familiar with writing their goals down. But what I need to stress here is that the basic but significant change, the metamorphosis that will ensure that you accomplish your goal, is truly visualizing what your mind is concentrated on. Imagine that single powerful focus as like the concentrated beam of sunlight through a magnifying glass that burns a hole in a piece of paper. Own that single-mindedness and then internalize it.

No one is going to be more passionate about you achieving the goal that you visualize than you. What do I mean? This is where toughness enters in. In your mind, you will wrestle with your internal GPS and the voice of skepticism or the suppressive voices of concern. Realizing your destination requires you to be resolute by grabbing the points to create a line to the destination within your mind. Truly, this is the exceptional part: I am a firm believer that if you can visualize the flight plan, if you can connect the mental dots in your brain, you will succeed. Let your brain fully comprehend and absorb the experience of where you want to go. With the grid coordinates plugged in, that determination and powerful mental imagery, nothing can stop you. I repeat: nothing can stop you.

Now, how do you progress from here? The key is that you need to do the work. You have the visualization. What are the steps you need to execute that will allow you to achieve this goal and be confident in the journey in front of you? Use the technique of reverse planning. Start from the goal, your visualization, and walk it back through each milestone. Start with what's required to get there and work back to the next step. This requires concentration and focus, but your brain will help. Stay with the visualization. Your brain will interpolate the rest. It will connect the dots.

You need to become a subject matter expert so you know all the inputs required—that is, bring your brain the content required to chart the course to your destination. Think of this as getting all the ingredients before you begin to bake. This will help you navigate on your forward path to meet your goal.

This concept was perhaps best said by General MacArthur during his speech to the West Point cadets: "They give you a temper of the will, a quality of the imagination, a vigor of the emotions, a freshness of the deep springs of life, a temperamental predominance of courage over timidity, *an appetite for adventure over love of ease* [italics added for emphasis]."[5]

---

5   MacArthur, General Douglas. "Duty, Honor, Country." Address at West Point Military Academy, New York, May 12, 1962.

CHAPTER 5 TAKEAWAYS

- To begin with the end in mind, to determine one's destiny, it must first emanate from within oneself. This impassioned feeling is simply the physical and mental alignment of where you want to be, the future projection of you.

- Building the first pillar of the Elite Performance Pillars™ consists of a commitment to take deliberate actions to be a better you.

- In life, there are things you can do, and then there are things that you want to do.

- If you are true to yourself and really focus, believe, and trust your internal GPS, it will set the path for the journey ahead.

- The Right-Angle Rule: There is the person in the mirror and God above. You must be honest with the man in the mirror, and the man above knows all. Use the Right-Angle Rule and be true to yourself when visualizing your career destination.

OWN THE MORNING, OWN YOUR LIFE

"The secret of your future can be found in your daily routine."
—MIKE MURDOCK

HOW YOU START your morning is your competitive advantage. This is the time of the day that's your sanctuary. A morning routine ensures that when you start the day, you start winning. In other words, you have an objective every day, and nothing gets in the way of you accomplishing this objective because it's the first thing you do.

It's really important that I stress this point that while, yes, there are many things outside of your control, few people truly maximize everything within their control. That is why you must maximize this time that is truly yours if you are going to be an elite performer. You are the designer and architect of your morning. I will provide you with a step-by-step guide in this chapter to start every morning with your mind, soul, and body at peak performance and to carry that positive momentum throughout your day.

You own your morning. This is in your area of responsibility (your AOR). This military term refers to a pre-defined region with specific geographic boundaries assigned to combatant commanders where they have the authority to plan and conduct operations for which a force or component commander bears a certain responsibility. This system is designed to allow a single commander to exercise command and control of all military forces in the AOR.

As an elite performer, you are the commander solely responsible for the daily morning mission. It is your area of responsibility. Remember that on this battlefield, you are in charge of your morning routine, and starting your day off right sets the tone for the rest of the day. Seize this moment each day, harnessing its power to build momentum and stack the odds in your favor. Embrace the philosophy of Nike and "Just Do It," and take charge of your routine with unwavering authority.

THE SIX-STEP ELITE PERFORMANCE MORNING ROUTINE

Before you enter your office or look at your email, this morning is yours. Managing you is the first leg of the tripod, and the goal is to be the best you that you can be. Having a positive mindset is a critical success factor for those who perform at the elite level. Developing a morning routine is the cornerstone of your foundation. I will share with you the elite performance morning routine (EPMR) that I have developed. The EPMR has six proven steps to make each of your mornings the best they can be. And if you own your morning, you own the day.

In my executive coaching business, I have researched elite performers across a diverse range of fields. From leading CEOs to top athletes, actors, military leaders, and pioneers of Silicon Valley, I have studied the strategies and habits that have made these individuals successful. By analyzing their approaches to leadership, performance, and personal growth, I aim to help my clients become the best versions of themselves.

Since I joined the military at the age of seventeen, I have embraced a morning routine that has become an integral part of my life. (To be fair, growing up as the son of a US Marine, my morning routine was somewhat enforced upon me) Getting up with a purpose was incumbent upon me from an early age, and my personal entry into the military solidified the permanent adaptation of EPMR in my life. Over the years, I have continuously improved and polished it, striving for perfection. I have observed that the top performers in any field have a consistent morning routine, and I firmly believe that starting the day off right sets the tone for success.

The best thing about your morning routine is that every day when you wake up, you and you alone determine the outcome of your morning. Immerse yourself in the transformative elite performance morning routine that will awaken your mind, nourish your spirit, bring harmony to your world, infuse your body with energy, and ignite your day with purpose. Experience the exhilaration of setting a clear vision for the day ahead and kick-starting each morning. Embrace this empowering routine and enjoy the satisfaction of successfully starting each day.

BUILD YOUR OWN WINNING STREAK EVERY MORNING

Winning streaks inspire and motivate and are sought after by every team that steps into arenas, fields, rinks, and stadiums worldwide. Witness the captivating tale of the Tampa Bay Rays, who, at the dawn of the 2023 baseball season, etched their names in history by tying the record of thirteen consecutive victories. Such a feat stands alongside the legendary 17–0 season of the Miami Dolphins in 1972, the only perfect season in NFL history. These awe-inspiring triumphs, attained by only a select few teams across the extensive chronicles of both sports, remind us of the boundless potential of human determination and teamwork. They serve as shining examples of what can be accomplished when dedication and excellence converge, fueling our own aspirations to reach new heights game by game, win by win.

How would you like to start your personal winning streak today? Invest in yourself with a morning routine and you can start with a win every day you wake up. The elite performance morning routine will allow you to start each morning 6–0. You will be on a winning streak before you walk out the door or head to your desk. Yes, if you do this every day for a month, your morning scoreboard will be 180–0. So, let's go.

Better yet, when you wake up tomorrow and execute your elite performance morning routine, you will extend your personal winning streak. Pillar I: Being a Better You, the initial step of the three-part Elite Performance Pillars™, is to empower yourself by taking control of your mornings, thereby claiming ownership of your life by building your own winning streak. To accomplish this, I encourage you to make a firm commitment to establishing your elite performance morning routine. By dedicating yourself to a structured morning regimen, you lay the foundation for a more productive, purposeful, and fulfilling life. Embrace this powerful practice and witness the transformative impact it can have on your overall well-being and success.

The mental advantage of starting every day with a "W" in the win–loss column sets you up for success daily. No matter what comes at you later in the day, the very first thing you did was for yourself, so you literally start the day as a winner. Invest in yourself with a morning routine and start with a win. Why is this so important? Because you will be challenged as you pursue your path, guided by your internal GPS.

As robust as I think I am, there were days in the past (and I recognize there will be more in the future) when, despite my military training, academic degrees, professional certifications, and innate grit, I was hit hard and life set me back on my heels or, a few times, right down to the canvas. It's not how many times you fall but how many times you get up that will determine your success. But, if I'm honest with you, in those moments when I found myself knocked down to the canvas, I really leaned on the precedent of success I had set up for myself with the EPMR. It was that fact-based action of encouragement that I planned for every morning.

Every morning, I hold myself accountable and I execute. This gives me self-confidence, the feeling that I got this or will get this; that I will apply the same discipline, resolve, and determination that I do to my EPMR; and that I will persevere and accomplish the challenges ahead or adapt and overcome, but I will continue my journey. I am a winner. Every morning, Lord willing, I will own my morning and perform my EPMR—the best investment I can make in myself every morning.

Now, there are many thoughts on how you can start your day. I mentioned that I researched a wide variety of successful people's morning routines, and here is one I'd like to share with you.

ELITE PERFORMANCE MORNING ROUTINE

One of the most-watched speeches on YouTube is about a morning routine. Some of you may be familiar with Admiral McRaven's commencement address given to the graduates of the University of Texas at Austin on May 17, 2014, titled "Make Your Bed." In his speech, he shared that every morning in basic SEAL training, his instructors, who at the time were all Vietnam veterans, would show up to his barracks room, and the first thing they would inspect was his bed. If he did it right, the corners would be square, the covers pulled tight, the pillow centered just under the headboard, and the extra blanket folded neatly at the foot of the rack.[6]

It was a simple task, mundane at best, but every morning, they were required to make their beds to perfection. It seemed a little ridiculous at the time, particularly in light of the fact that they were aspiring to be real warriors, tough battle-hardened SEALs, but the wisdom of this simple act has been proven many times over: If you make your bed every morning, you will have accomplished the first task of the day. It will give you a small sense of pride, and it will encourage you to do another task and another and another. By the end of the day, that one task completed will have turned into many tasks completed. Making your bed will also reinforce the fact that little things in life matter. If you can't do the little things right, you'll never do the big things right.

That's why I'm adamant about the elite performance morning routine. You start with one objective in the morning: you make your bed and you accomplish it. This internal momentum builds, and you are on to the next step in your morning routine and the next. By the time you start your workday, you've already built up a tremendous amount of momentum. Not only do you feel it internally, but what's internalized is externalized. Other people see that sense of accomplishment and preparedness and the level of quiet confidence that you are ready to excel today.

TO BE ELITE, YOU NEED TO SLEEP

There are additional thoughts on what time one should start the day. What is most important is to commit to your EPMR by simply going to bed thirty minutes earlier and getting up thirty minutes earlier. The next question you may

---

6   UT News, "Adm. McRaven Urges Graduates to Find Courage to Save the World," The University of Texas at Austin, May 16, 2014, https://news.utexas. edu/2014/05/16/mcraven-urges-graduates-to-find-courage-to-change-the-world/.

have is about how much sleep you need. Irrefutably, sleep is one of the most important factors in your performance and overall health. The amount of sleep you need depends on many different factors, including your age, genetics, and how well you sleep at night. Nevertheless, a target of seven to eight hours per night for adults is the consensus. You may be comfortable with sleeping less than seven hours a night, but sleep plays such a vital role in maintaining good health and well-being that you should try to get at least seven hours.[7] During sleep, your body works to support healthy brain function and maintain your physical health. Sleep also helps your brain regulate emotions. During sleep, your body is hard at work repairing itself by releasing proteins and hormones that help restore damaged tissues, including muscles. So, if you want to be elite, you need your sleep.

Elite performers manage their schedules so they get the minimum seven hours of sleep per night. If you also do that, you'll be ready to invest in yourself with a morning routine and start every day with a "W." Prepare your mental state to succeed and take control of the things you can control. I will share my EPMR with you so you can adopt your own morning routine and permanently change your life by making a thirty-minute investment in yourself each day.

To achieve excellence, the key element of your morning routine and many of the other elite performance building blocks is the commitment to small, seemingly insignificant, daily improvements done consistently over time to yield staggering results. My strongest suggestion is that you start changing your life today and implement an EPMR.

Why do you need an EPMR? Remind yourself that you own the morning, so start your day calmly. Feed your spirit

7   Danielle Pacheco and Abhinav Singh, "Sleep Calculator: Your Personalized Tool for Sleep," Sleep Foundation, accessed November 12, 2023, https://www.sleepfoundation.org/sleep-calculator.

first. Don't plug into the digital world. Instead, take a few minutes to read the Bible, meditate, do some deep breathing, or simply sit in silence. Be thankful today is a new day—your first win of the day.

For the body, there's no better way to start your day than with a glass of water. Hydrate the system and perform a minimum of fifteen minutes of exercise to stimulate the body. A fifteen-minute, no-interruption workout is plenty of time to build strength and increase flexibility and endurance.

I've included some simple no-excuse exercises on my website that can be done in any small room or outdoor space (please go to *www.execpathfinders.com/insights* to find a list). There is an infinite number of things you can do to get a good workout in fifteen minutes. Trust me, in fifteen minutes, you burn calories, get a good heart rate going, and gain strength. You can do EMOM (every minute on the minute) exercise or have an excellent yoga or tai chi session so that you really put up a solid W for yourself and accomplish this objective.

It doesn't matter if you do yoga, stretching, high-intensity interval training (HIIT), weight training, sports training, squash, pickleball, or an early morning swim. You need at least fifteen minutes to awaken the body and energize it. This gets your blood pumping, and most importantly, gives you a sense of accomplishment. That's the one thing you own. So, right away on the scorecard of life, you are building your personal winning streak to 3–0. Your mindset is positive. You set out to incorporate the elite performance morning routine into your daily life, and you did it.

Momentum is now on your side. This key element of discipline really sets you up for success every day. Protect that time and own it so that, before anything from the work world or personal life can interrupt you, you've already won.

This will help shape your brand. *How?* you may ask. People will get to know you have a routine. This implies discipline. They will know you get up early in the morning. Reinforce your commitment to your goals, and you'll have a results-oriented mindset.

I have instilled this discipline in my routine, getting one win each morning, throughout my entire life. Starting in the morning with getting the body and mind going is really the best chance for preparation and success.

You may be wondering how long it will take to make your EPMR a habit. You may guess that it takes three to four weeks from what you have heard or read. If you dig a little deeper into the scientific evidence, you will find that Maxwell Maltz, a plastic surgeon in the 1950s, began noticing a strange pattern among his patients. When Dr. Maltz would perform an operation (e.g., facial cosmetic surgery) he found that it would take the patient about twenty-one days to get used to seeing their new face. He also observed a similar time frame applied when a patient had an arm or leg amputated. He noticed that the patient would sense a phantom limb for about twenty-one days before adjusting to the new situation. Dr. Maltz then thought about how long it took him to adjust to change. He found it also took about twenty-one days for him to form a new habit. In 1960, Dr. Maltz wrote a book called *Psycho-Cybernetics*, in which he observes, "These, and many other commonly observed phenomena tend to show that it requires a minimum of about 21 days for an old mental image to dissolve and a new one to jell."[8] The book went on to become a great success, selling more than thirty million copies.

However, this is when the problem started. The idea

8   Maltz, Maxwell. *Psycho-Cybernetics: Updated and Expanded.* TarcherPerigree, 2015.

that it took twenty-one days to form a habit quickly spread. Over the decades, the myth spawned a large number of self-help books from authors like Zig Ziglar, Brian Tracy, and Tony Robbins. That's understandable since three weeks to form a habit is convenient, just long enough to be believable and just short enough to be achievable.

To be elite, we must be realistic. The old saying applies here: if it sounds too good to be true, it's probably not true. Let's look at what the science says. Phillippa Lally is a health psychology researcher at University College London. In a study published in the *European Journal of Social Psychology*, Lally and her research team figured out just how long it actually takes to form a new habit: an average of sixty-six days.[9] So, despite what you may have heard or read, it will probably take you just over two months to build a new behavior into your life, not twenty-one days. But the message is the same. Substantial changes are a result of making small changes consistently over time (expect two to eight months to realize significant results).

No excuses. Today is the first day to start. Wake up, rock it, and repeat. Commit to the ritual of the EPMR and win every morning. The six steps of the EPMR are described below.

THE ELITE PERFORMANCE MORNING ROUTINE:

STEP 1: MORNING REFLECTION/FEED THE SPIRIT
- Go to bed thirty minutes earlier. After sleeping seven hours, wake up to start your magical thirty-minute EPMR.

---

9   UCL, "How long does it take to form a habit?" University College London, August 4, 2009, https://www.ucl.ac.uk/news/2009/aug/how-long-does-it-take-form-habit.

- Rise with the sun (or even before it) as part of your brand. Waking up early can help you feel more productive and focused throughout the day.
- Own your morning, own your life. Reward yourself and enjoy this personal solitude. Tell yourself, "Let go of what's gone, be grateful for what remains, and look forward to what is coming next."
- Feed your spirit. Do not plug into the digital world. Instead, take a few minutes to read the Bible, meditate, do some deep breathing, or simply sit in silence. Your first win of the day: 1–0.

STEP 2: MAKE YOUR BED; SET YOUR WORLD IN ORDER

- Determine the first thing you will do every morning when you get out of bed. For me, I stand tall and stretch, arms to the sky, and take a deep breath. Then, I reach down to my toes and do a walkout, followed by thirty-four push-ups. That way, I'm more than one-third of the way to one hundred push-ups just minutes into my day.
- Or you can follow the Navy commander's SEAL routine and make your bed, hug your partner or dog or cat, complete the sun salutation sequence of yoga poses, or brush your teeth standing on one leg. Whatever you do in the morning, make it a ritual that marks the start of a new day, a fresh start, and a win for you! 2–0!

STEP 3: **DRINK WATER**

- Replenish: drinking water as soon as you wake up replenishes your body with the hydration that it needs to properly function.
- Flush out toxins: water helps flush out toxins and keeps your body hydrated, which is vital for the proper functioning of internal organs.
- Nurture: drinking water in the morning also refreshes your mind because your brain has a high concentration of water. Water is fuel for your brain. Without it, you can feel drained and suffer from low energy levels and reduced cognitive function. So, drink up—water, that is! 3–0.

STEP 4: **MORNING EXERCISE**

- Start the heart: exercising in the morning for fifteen minutes every day will help you feel more energized, improve decision-making, and increase productivity and focus throughout the day.
- Your body's circadian rhythm can also benefit from morning exercise, enabling you to have better quality sleep at night.
- Without morning exercise, you delay the full awakening of your body and all the inherent benefits thereof. Maximize everything in your AO (area of operations). That is what elite performers do. 4–0.

STEP 5: **BE THANKFUL**

- Take a few minutes to say "thank you" for all the things you would miss in your life if they were gone tomorrow. This is a great way to put things in perspective each day. 5–0.

STEP 6: **PLAN YOUR DAY/PLAN YOUR WEEK**

- Plan your day with a clear mind. Winning starts at the beginning. The wisest way to guarantee that you consistently perform at elite levels is to instill a habitual routine. 6–0.

Shortly, I will introduce the magical five-minute technique, but as you are just adopting the EPMR, we first need to establish your core life goals so you can better manage you. Ideally, find a time of solitude early on a weekend morning to check in with yourself. Block off a one-hour period. To be most effective, follow steps one through five above and do not engage with any digital or outside interruptions. I will not be there, but I trust that if you want to be an elite performer and change your life, you will heed my advice.

This next step is the key differentiator that we discussed earlier in the book. Taking the bold step of dedicating 5–10 percent of your time to managing yourself and planning your career establishes the groundwork for you to accelerate your career.

I didn't realize this powerful career and life transformer until the golden decades of my career. It has amazing power. It makes a huge difference to simply shut things off, find a quiet time where you will ideally not be interrupted, and unleash your brain power. You will truly be amazed at how clearly, quickly, and succinctly you can think, and what you can accomplish in one hour when focused on you.

Everyone is probably familiar with the management philosophy that if you fail to plan, you plan to fail. Then why is it that so few of us take the time to plan our own careers? Nearly every executive and senior manager I meet acknowledges that they should spend time managing their career. However, when I ask them if they've spent thirty minutes or more in the last week to do so, nearly all of them say they haven't (with the predominant exception being those who have a coach). So, why is it that so many executives know it's important but so few act on it? What lurks underneath this apathy to take control of one's career is usually one or a mix of the following misconceptions: (1) the hidden belief that delivering results and meeting or exceeding your targets will be enough; (2) the assumption that the firm or management will recognize your contributions and will develop your career path for you; and (3) the idea that you are not political, so the large excuse blanket is tossed over the career-planning void, and the implicit belief is that you will leave it to faith or chance. Don't make the mistake of telling yourself that managing your career implies you're being political. You own your career, and managing your career is your responsibility. Managing your career is not about playing politics, it's about you developing and owning your career plans.

Grab your watch or the timer on your phone and set it for sixty minutes. I do not care how good of an expert marksman you may be. If you do not have a target or goal, or if you do not know where the target is, you cannot hit it. You are essentially shooting in the dark trying to improve.

Let's be SMARTer than that. To begin, I have a variation of the SMART acronym: simple and specific, measurable, achievable, relevant, and time-bound goals. In 2018, the MIT Sloan School of Management produced a white paper. Donald and Charles Sull made the case for a new acronym to help us set tangible goals: FAST, which stands for frequently reviewed, ambitious, specific, and transparent.[10] I believe FAST is better adapted to the pace of business today and the best fit for elite performers. The first change is frequently reviewing, which is critical to sustain momentum and avoid a slide at the offsite that doesn't get reviewed until the next offsite. Achievable is okay if your goal is to meet the standard, but if you want to make an impact, be bold and ambitious. Transparency, widely sharing what you seek to do (i.e., promoting your personal brand—more to come on this later), is powerful. You want peers, management, and direct reports to know your goals, and making your commitments public is a surefire way to keep your eyes on the prize.

When adopting FAST goals, I want you to keep it simple and think of no more than three to five. When your mind is focused and not in an environment with constant interruptions, you'll start to unleash its full power. Keep it simple and concise. Too many people make the mistake of coming up with long complex goals that they simply cannot remember. My rule is that when you achieve one goal, you can always add another, but having focus is a big contributor to success. So, keep it simple and focused.

Here is the exercise: As the pilot in command of your career, look out through the windshield of the aircraft. What are the things that are important to you? What are

10 Donald Sull and Charles Sull, "With Goals, FAST Beats SMART," MIT Sloan Management Review, June 5, 2018, https://sloanreview.mit.edu/article/with-goals-fast-beats-smart/; Steve Preda and Gregory Cleary, *Pinnacle*

the three to five simple goals you want to accomplish? Be instinctive. Set a timer for five minutes and reset it three or four times (corresponding to the number of goals). During each five-minute interval, write down one simple, measurable, achievable, relevant, and time-bound goal, but apply the FAST technique to ensure your goal can be frequently reviewed, is ambitious, is specific and transparent, and can be accomplished within twelve months.

Next, what are you trying to accomplish not only in your professional life but in your personal and family life, your fitness and spiritual goals, and your hobbies? Repeat the same exercise for the next three categories for fifteen minutes each. The finished product is a four-by-eight matrix.

I have enclosed an example of my elite performance matrix below for your visual reference. In the first column, I have four topics: spiritual, business (my two companies), family, and physical. In the next column, I have three to five simple FAST goals for each. In the last column, I've written down the next six months so I can denote progress and key milestones under each month's heading. My elite performance matrix is printed out and taped to the side of the printer that faces my desk. I have a pdf of the matrix on my phone and another copy on a small bulletin board under the poster of a motorbike that says, "Achieving good performance is a journey, not a destination."

ELITE PERFORMANCE MATRIX
2024 GOALS

SPIRITUAL	• EPMR, Read The Bible Daily • Parent's Bible Study • US Marines Church Support Group	AUG SEP OCT NOV DEC JAN
EXECPATH-FINDERS	• XX Clients • Book Launch • Thought Leaders Video Series • Keynote Speaker	AUG SEP OCT NOV DEC JAN
STARK CAPITAL	• Real Estate • INT'l 2 Exits and 1 Remodel • Private Equity - 5 Early-stage Investments • Liquid Markets Trading $XXk Qtrly	
FAMILY	• Wife Friday Dates • University Son Monthly Dinner • High School Son College Planning and Swimming • Thanksgiving, Christmas Plans	AUG SEP OCT NOV DEC JAN
PHYSICAL	• Center, PsP, PuP, ABS Daily • 45 Days for 45 Min Daily • Surf, Ski, Golf	AUG SEP OCT NOV DEC JAN

- Magical morning five-minute technique (six days a week): you've just completed the first five steps of your EPMR, and now you have five minutes to reflect upon your life goals, neatly summarized in an elite performance four-by-eight matrix. Take advantage of these magical few minutes. Unleash your brain power in the solitude of the morning and you'll be able to operate at full throttle.

- Row by row, take a quick inventory—a mark to market—of each of the foundational topics and related goals for managing you. Ask yourself how you are doing. Celebrate the small wins, and focus your efforts today on where you deem they are most needed. Reflect on the past twenty-four hours and determine where to focus your efforts today. That way, you have a game plan before you even go to work. You are an elite performer.

- It is best to perform any critical analyses in the morning, when your powers of logic and deduction are at their sharpest, because there is less interruption and your cognitive bandwidth is at its maximum. From this point onward, your cognitive processing capabilities deteriorate throughout the day. According to a study by scientists who have tracked how cognitive abilities rise and fall, most of our brains follow a predictable pattern of cognition that fluctuates hour by hour throughout the course of a day. [11] They found that speed and accuracy at completing tasks are better in the morning and that the ability to remain alert tracks closely with sleep.

---

11   Pink, Daniel H. *When: The Scientific Secrets of Perfect Timing.* Penguin, 2018.

- Plan for the week. I strongly recommend spending thirty minutes at least once a week reflecting on your goals, milestones accomplished, areas that require attention, and corrective actions and recording key progress made. Reevaluate goals as needed. Set your sights with a clear mind and update your matrix for the week ahead.

Add it up and you are now dedicating one hour a week in your EPMR to managing your career and life. You are doing this at the optimal time for your brain—in the morning when you are without digital distraction and at peak cognitive processing. You are adding to your personal winning streak. You made your bed or did some other useful activity, got the body started and hydrated, fed your soul, and gave thanks for those things you cherish.

You have proactively taken control of your life, not only by planning your career but by holistically taking care and paying attention to all of you. Each day, the experience will be richer. Your brain will process more, giving you time to reflect and reposition. And if you continue to perform the EPMR, you know that in a few months to just less than a year it will be a habit, a powerful, life-changing habit that will significantly help you gain perspective and inner confidence.

This has been one of the strongest contributors to my personal foundation, allowing me to manage me, and now you to manage you. You are adding tools to your personal tool kit, investing in yourself every morning to be the best possible you. As I mentioned before, my intention is to distill essential lessons from my lifetime and career, insights that took me years to master, internalize, and, in some instances, discover. I'm driven to share these invaluable career secrets with you so that you can adapt them in your own unique manner at the earliest opportunity. My aim is to empower you with the knowledge and wisdom to accelerate your own journey, allowing you to bypass potential obstacles and achieve your goals more swiftly. Embrace these lessons and unleash your full potential, starting from the very beginning of your own path to success. Would you like to work less and accomplish more? Let's get started on the next chapter.

CHAPTER 6 TAKEAWAYS

- The best thing about your morning routine is that every day when you wake up, you and you alone determine the outcome of your morning. You are the designer and the architect of your morning.

- The elite performance morning routine has six proven steps to make each of your mornings the best they can be. And if you own your morning, you own the day. It's the best investment you can make in yourself every day.
  - Step 1: Morning Reflection/Feed the Spirit
  - Step 2: Make Your Bed, Set Your World in Order
  - Step 3: Drink Water
  - Step 4: Morning Exercise
  - Step 5: Be Thankful
  - Step 6: Plan Your Day/Plan Your Week

- Have three to five FAST (frequently reviewed, ambitious, specific, and transparent) goals for each life category. I have four categories: spiritual, business, family, and physical.

FOCUS YIELDS RESULTS

"The secret of change is to focus all of your energy not on fighting the old, but on building the new."
—DAN MILLMAN

THE 2022 MOVIE *Everything Everywhere All at Once* is a very highly acclaimed film, but it's no way to run your life. The first thing I'll tell you is that you need to work less to accomplish more. Running nonstop on the treadmill of life may make you feel like you're working hard and focused on results, but you're not being strategic.

Do you think your boss is busy or that your boss's boss is busy? They have the same constraints as you—God gives each of us only twenty-four hours in a day. If you aspire to take on more responsibility, you have to prioritize, delegate, and partner effectively (we'll discuss this more in Pillar II: Being a Better Manager, which covers a more productive way to delegate). As an elite performer, how do we make the most out of each day, not only for our career but for our well-being and work-life balance?

THREE STEPS TO FOCUS YOUR DAYS
Step 1: Starting tomorrow, record how you spend every thirty minutes of your workday in bullet points on a simple spreadsheet. You can extend this exercise to before and after work to develop a fuller and richer understanding of your life, holistically. The first thirty minutes of every day should be easy. It is your thirty-minute elite performance morning routine. You can also complete the exercise for the time after

work until you go to bed. At a minimum, record how you spend every half hour of your workday for one week.

Step 2: Review your weekly activities. This goal is twofold. The first aim is to limit each day's tasks so you can fully commit yourself to the tasks you choose. The second is to ask yourself the following questions for each task: Is this the best use of my time? Can this task be reassigned? Can I attend this meeting less frequently or have a deputy attend in my place?

Step 3: Complete your review and adjust your schedule to free up a minimum of 5 percent of your time to manage your career. For example, if you work fifty-hour work weeks, you need to free up two and a half hours. Find this time and block it off in your schedule. One schedule item you may consider that worked well for me throughout my career was blocking out one hour every Sunday after the day's activities but before dinner.

Here is the rhythm you seek as an elite performer. Concentrate on fewer FAST objectives and build momentum as you complete the objectives. With greater focus, you will improve your efficiency and reinforce your sense of accomplishment. That is why we limited ourselves to three to five goals for each major subject matter in Chapter 6. Focus yields results. Focus on less, get more done, and when you finish one, add the next objective.

Visualize starting a run on a treadmill. As you turn it on, you set your speed. There is a lag as the treadmill starts to slowly pick up speed and your pace starts to quicken. The digits on the digital display increase more quickly as you get into your pace, hitting your stride. We are creating the same environment for success for you now. Focus deeply, achieve efficiently, and build speed by adding the next objective but keeping your focus and discipline tight. Speed is important as you derive two benefits: you will be seen as someone who gets things done and your own self-satisfaction at accomplishing tasks will increase, which will release endorphins and provide you with positive reinforcement.

Far too many people delude themselves. Not only do they waste time on non-essential tasks but they hurt their reputations. People remember the ball you dropped, not the eight you were juggling. Every act you commit needs to be with foresight and purpose. We are building a rock-solid base with a proven methodology for starting each day as a winner mentally, physically, and spiritually.

We are now making sure that in our seventeen hours (twenty-four hours minus seven sleep hours) we are exactly aware of how we spend our time each day. Maintaining a strong resolve is crucial in avoiding any distractions that may divert your attention from achieving your goals. Stop deluding yourself and be resolute in your focus as you purposefully build your brand, brick by brick.

Resist the temptation of trying to be exhaustive and drowning in endless to-do lists. In the military, when you go on a live-fire assault course, the principle is simple. The targets closest to you are the ones that pose the greatest threat to you, so you must engage them first. To instill this discipline, the silhouettes nearest you pop up for the shortest period of time. The takeaway is that in your day-to-day life, you must stay focused on the critical mission, have a well-defined and succinct list of objectives, focus, engage, and move forward.

Oftentimes, when you set large, complex, multilayered goals, it is hard to continue making progress because it can feel like you are trying to push a large boulder up a hill with little signs of progress. Instead, break the big boulder into smaller goals, the ones to your front that you can see and engage in. Build momentum. By breaking the complex goal into smaller goals, you can make visible progress toward your end goal.

THE SWEET SPOT OF THREE TO FIVE GOALS

Staying focused on your three to five key objectives will allow your mind to operate at the optimal level, its efforts deeply concentrated on the most important objectives. Do not be distracted by long lists that your mind cannot even remember, where instead of focusing on problem-solving and determining the path ahead, your cognitive processes are stuck in neutral trying to recall superfluous information.

Science also supports this, as the bandwidth number or the capacity of short-term memory is often referred to as the "magical number seven." This concept was first introduced by psychologist George A. Miller in his 1956 paper "The Magical Number Seven, Plus or Minus Two: Some Limits on Our Capacity for Processing Information." The study found that an average person can typically process only about seven units of information at any given time, however, this number can vary depending on the individual.[12] I like to err on the side of caution. Throughout my program, I suggest you focus on no more than three to five objectives, both for personal mastery and for professional development, and cascade this down to your N-1s.

Instill this discipline and you will build a reputation that you do what you say, are consistent, are organized, and demonstrate the mettle to take on more responsibility

12   Marie Doorey, "George A. Miller," *Encyclopedia Brittanica*, July 18, 2023, https://www.britannica.com/biography/George-A-Miller#ref1200615.

because you are goal focused. This is also an important step for building your brand. Everyone is busy, but by keeping a short list of objectives, you'll dramatically increase people's probability of remembering what you do, your goals, and your impact on the organization. A good friend of mine simply said, "Don't try to boil the ocean." With this mindset, you can build a strong brand and establish yourself as a trustworthy and capable individual.

Let's go to work. What are your three to five business or corporate goals? Are they written down? Does your boss know what they are? Your peers? Your N-1s? Your team? If not, what do you think this implies about your brand? Is there clarity around your sense of purpose, your tenacity, and your focus on execution? Now, the litmus test: If you don't have three to five objectives, put this book down and write them down now. This ties into your EPMR. The four-by-eight matrix with three to five objectives for each of your core categories will neatly fit on half a sheet of paper. Then, your life game plan will be at the ready. Take a picture of it, print it out, and post it near your desk. Your ability to focus on a goal and visually see it will dramatically increase your chances of achieving it. When it comes to achievement, in your business or personal life, you must stay persistent to make it happen.

BUILDING YOU

Picture that you are constructing a building. This building is you. Each of the categories and objectives is a core part of the foundation. Picture the corners of your building, anchored with your key life categories. The carefully laid bricks around them are the three to five objectives for each that you are fully focused on (for me, the foundation is composed of these cornerstones: spiritual, business, family, and physical, then the next layer is the objectives for each). Where you spend your time relates to the bricks you lay to build your personal brand. To build a strong brand that is easily recognizable, you need to be consistent. You are building your personal brand that is directly linked to you. What is your personal brand? It's what is said about you and what people believe about you when you are not in the room.

You are the architect of you. The building you are constructing requires a plan. It requires you, as the architect and main contractor, to dedicate 5–10 percent of your time to plan your brand and your career. This plan is the careful integration of the Right Angle Rule of being true to yourself and ensuring that the ingredients of your brand on the outside accurately reflect the contents inside.

WHAT IS YOUR BRAND?

I built my brand over the years from the different work experiences in my career. Starting with my military days, I learned to be purposeful: train to the standard, not to the time allocated. Those who served with me knew my mantra: "Don't fill time because there is a four-hour block of instruction. Instead, define the standard we seek to achieve and train until we achieve that standard."

In my finance career, I adopted a client-driven brand. I fostered a strong commitment to being client-focused in everything I did. It also included positive tenacity built by exhibiting a strong work ethic and executing the plan consistently, underscored by a positive outlook.

Your brand is how you are perceived by the outside world based on your inner focus. If you want to achieve your more difficult strategic goals, you need to instill discipline and work on your brand every day. Ultimately, where and how you spend your time will determine your brand. As

George Lucas of *Star Wars* fame said, "Always remember, your focus determines your reality."[13]

Elite performers do not spend time focusing on what could go wrong. Instead, they focus their efforts on ensuring it goes right. Elite performers will have no more than three to five goals per subject area, and they will conserve their energy by not getting stuck on what can go wrong. Instead, they'll dig in and commit 100 percent of their focus to achieving their desired outcome.

DIGITAL MAYHEM

The realities of the digital age are vast. The preference for multitasking should be anything but, and I fought this battle personally for many years. I was a digital victim. The human brain was not designed to operate at its optimal level with the continual interruptions of the digital era. I told myself as a pilot that multitasking was my strength, but this simply wasn't true. It took courage to dedicate time to focus and reduce the barrage of digital interruption, but if you have the courage to try, I will guarantee you a positive outcome. As an elite performer, you must be disciplined and eliminate the distractions of the digital world; the constant text messages, emails, application notifications, and social media interruptions make it hard to stay focused on anything. Block out periods in your calendar so that you are not interrupted when you are dedicating time to managing your career. The same goes for work blocks dedicated to your tightly defined objectives: set your timer for thirty minutes, turn your ringer off, ignore your emails, and get focused.

By singularly focusing on one goal, you will be much clearer in thought, and your mind will run in fifth gear. Void

13 Rhett Power, "How to Focus Like George Lucas," *Forbes*, May 3, 2020, https://www.forbes.com/sites/rhettpower/2020/05/03/how-to-focus-like-george-lucas/?sh=73a5b8f1510b.

of distractions, it will be in the optimal environment to process at peak performance. Lastly, choose a time to look at your email after your career management time. This will calm the subliminal concerns your brain may have and provide a calming effect, since you know you have dedicated a block of time to addressing your inbox. The bottom line is that your personal brand depends on you mastering your environment.

The next part of the exercise is where you need to do some self-reflection using the Right-Angle Rule combined with self-awareness and the final step of strategically aligning your brand with your manager's goals, the firm's goals, and your personal attributes.

I will share with you the development of my brand in my financial career as a young managing director at a large European bank. In those days, I was managing a medium-sized team on the trading floor. The days were long and intense in the late 1990s. There was an exhilarating energy throughout the day as we were in the formation of the overzealousness of the first tech bubble. Everything was go, go, go. The pace was nonstop, and often, you were running just to keep up.

Two days a week, from 6:30 to 7:30 p.m., we had French language training in a meeting room off the trading floor. I took German throughout high school, but the basic rules of German seemed to be the antithesis of French. What is verbalized in German was silent in French, and my attention span at the end of the day was nearly depleted. However, this was just one component. As I looked around, some of my colleagues did everything they could to fit in, not only through mastering the language part but also through culture, hobbies, cuisine, and wine. Many shared a similar educational background with one another, but this was something I was never going to be able to mimic. I could not turn back the hands of time and change my educational background. I liked the bank and truly believed it had amazing potential, but I could not see a successful career path if I was simply trying to fit in by mimicking others, since I would never measure up to their standard. So, the fundamental question was how to be true to the Right-Angle Rule. What were the innate, unique qualities that I had that could allow me to contribute value to the bank? How could I play to my strengths and align myself with the goals of my manager and the firm?

Scarcity value was the positioning that made sense. The large institutional US clients were a significant growth opportunity for the bank, so becoming a conduit between the bank and the US clients would become my personal brand. Here, my upbringing in the United States, my educational background, and my shared cultural experience, coupled with a strong understanding of the bank's capabilities and culture, allowed me to be a conduit between the two actors and create a win-win opportunity for both parties. Making client focus part of my personal brand fit the bill. The client part of the business was something I was passionate about. I had pride in the bank and knew it had unique capabilities sought out by US clients. I was well-positioned to connect the two with an equitable value proposition. The US market was the top priority for growth, and the firm was keen to develop its client franchise and needed managers who could execute this mission. My manager was the senior person in charge of developing the client business, and I was keen to do everything I could to help him be successful in doing so.

Your brand takes forethought, must leverage who you are, and ideally fit a strategic need for your boss and the firm. The key is that you need to link what your manager is asking of you and what your manager's boss is asking of them. Find this intersection and align your personal brand with it.

Build your brand brick by brick. Your three to five objectives build the foundation. The Right-Angle Rule is the filter of effectiveness and authenticity. Develop your mantra so that you project your brand (backed up by actions). We will discuss the Push and Pull Rule later in the book, but for now, what you want to create is the pull from management. The next time there is a town hall or an offsite meeting, management may "pull" you into the agenda because they understand your brand—what your value add is to the firm, supported by your actions and accomplishments of the supporting objectives—and that your brand is aligned with management's objectives up the chain of command. This does not happen by accident, so start planning and developing your brand now.

"IT DOES WHAT IT SAYS ON THE TIN"

This may sound funny to you just as it did to me the first time I heard it in London. "It does what it says on the tin" means that it does what it says on the label. If it says "baked beans" on the tin, then you'll find baked beans inside. It may sound simple, but being amazingly predictable is a key attribute that we will discuss in more detail in Pillar III: Managing Your Manager.

I grew fond of this British saying over my nearly three decades in the UK. As an employee in the firm, you and all the other employees are like cans in a store. Some cans have a prominent position at the end of the aisle, and their cans are well-branded, well-known, and well-understood. They have credibility and brand power because, like the British saying, the brand promoted is consistent with the person (the contents) within. Other brands in the store are generic titles—data analyst, systems engineer, institutional salesperson—but not uniquely developed brands. People walk by the generic brands, which go unnoticed. They are just another fill-in-the-blank salesperson, engineer, and so on. Somewhere in a corner of the store are the dented tins and perhaps a few tins without labels—the brandless tins. No one knows what is inside. Sometimes, someone will take a marker and write "Beans," but skepticism prevails, and you're not really sure what is inside—it could be caviar, or it could be sauerkraut.

As I said earlier, neither the HR partner nor your manager are there to manage your career. Most likely, they are not going to take the onus upon themselves to develop your brand. On too many occasions, I have seen people in middle management positions discussed in absentia during a people performance review behind closed doors become the brandless tin. Few people know their identity, their brand, or what they deliver to the firm. You do not want to be the brandless tin—nameless, faceless. Perhaps you deliver the results, but management doesn't understand your brand, your unique selling point (USP).

Taking ownership of your personal brand and investing in its development is an essential factor in achieving excellence in any field. By establishing a distinct identity and showcasing your unique strengths and skills, you can differentiate yourself from others and stand out as an elite performer. Whether you are an entrepreneur, a freelancer, or a corporate executive, building a strong personal brand can help you establish credibility, gain recognition, and attract new opportunities. Take the time to define your brand vision, craft your messaging, and leverage various channels to promote yourself and your expertise. With a clear and compelling personal brand, you can elevate your career and achieve success on your own terms.

JEKYLL AND HYDE

The consistency of your brand is paramount. There is no Jekyll and Hyde. You are you, so be honest with yourself, and be consistent.

We all know those people who are habitually a few minutes late for meetings, either due to some level of inflated self-importance or simply a lack of basic discipline. We also witness the people who consistently miss deadlines, deliver less-than-comprehensive project work, or miss the basic big-picture check-in: do my numbers make sense?

When Mr. Hyde leaves work and walks into the house, does he experience a metamorphosis, turning into Dr. Jekyll, someone punctual and reliable who goes the extra mile? If you were in a crisis and had one phone call, would this person be at the top of your list? There is no on-and-off in terms of your conduct, personal standards, punctuality, job excellence, or exerting your absolute best effort in everything within your area of responsibility. Own this. The simple commitment to consistency and self-accountability will transform your life if you decide to look in the mirror today and set the standard that becomes your brand. How do people describe you? Is their perception aligned with what you want it to be, what you aspire to be, and what you can be with a simple commitment and elimination of Jekyll and Hyde? To put this all together, there are no illusions. There is no Jekyll and Hyde, and the Right-Angle Rule is a constant. You are what is seen in the mirror and what is known by God above.

CHAPTER 7 **TAKEAWAYS**

- Manage your time. Start tomorrow and record how you spend every thirty minutes of your workday in bullet points on a simple spreadsheet. (The first thirty minutes every day should be easy. It's your thirty-minute elite performance morning routine.)

- Commit 5-10 percent of your time to managing your career. Complete your review and adjust your schedule to free up that minimum of 5 percent.

- Own your brand. Build your personal brand brick by brick. Your three to five objectives build the foundation. The Right-Angle Rule is the filter of effectiveness and authenticity. Develop your mantra so that you project your brand (backed up by deliberate actions).

PART III

PILLAR II: BEING A BETTER MANAGER

LEAD LIKE MACARTHUR

"A true leader has the confidence to stand alone, the courage to make tough decisions, and the compassion to listen to the needs of others. He does not set out to be a leader but becomes one by the equality of his actions and the integrity of his intent."
—GENERAL DOUGLAS MACARTHUR

CONGRATULATIONS! YOU HAVE completed the first pillar of the Elite Performance Pillars™, improving yourself by investing 5–10 percent of your time in proactively managing your career.

You have:

- Developed an elite performance morning routine;

- Put the Right-Angle Rule to work;

- Implemented three to five FAST objectives to build the foundation of you; and

- Built your personal brand.

Being the best "you" allows you to be a better manager. You are the foundation of your career. Like constructing a building, your career must have a strong foundation built on bedrock. No matter what point you're at in your career, you have to ensure your foundation is robust. Your foundation is now strengthened by three actions you have deliberately decided to take: adding the elite performance morning routine, ensuring that your career can grow confidently tall by adhering to the Right-Angle Rule, and investing time in managing your career instead of expending all of your time in task-execution mode.

One of my clients, a senior health care executive, found that one key change—taking the time to manage his career and think strategically—served as a significant catalyst that profoundly changed the trajectory of his firm. Prior to working together, he had many direct reports, actively managed many aspects of the business, and moved from task to task, but he did not have time to analyze or think strategically. During our initial discussions to define the scope of our consulting and coaching engagement, he expressed that his goal was to grow the firm's top line by ten times what it was. The executive and I had already known each other for over a decade, and I always admired his work ethic and tenacity to get things done.

Over the short span of six years, he built one of the premier home health care companies on the East Coast and did so through the extremely challenging COVID-19 period of 2020–2022. I was excited to work with him on this ambitious goal and shared my Elite Performance Pillars™ program with him. I introduced him to Pillar I and asked him to do the same exercise that you just did, to record how he spent his time each day in half-hour blocks for one week. He sent me the results, and we discussed them during our next executive coaching session. This simple step of recording how he spent his time, and then stepping back with me to review it, was quite revealing. His days were overbooked. He had too many direct reports that he was still managing personally. Additionally, he oversaw the banking and accounting functions and served as the pseudo-head of HR. Also, all of the new client leads were coming directly to him.

As we discussed how he was spending time going from task to task, he began to realize that the company needed oxygen to grow. Just like they say during the briefing on an airplane, when the oxygen masks drop, you have to save yourself first so you're able to save others. He needed oxygen and time to breathe, to look above the horizon, and to focus on his number one objective, which was growth. He realized he was unintentionally smothering the growth the company was so desperately trying to achieve.

We took the first step and blocked out 10 percent of his time for managing his career, including the one hour a week we were spending together in our executive coaching session. Most importantly, this meeting served as a catalyst for him to make organizational changes and free up his time to meet the dedicated 5–10 percent career management time requirement outlined in Pillar I. It served as a mechanism for him to make the organizational changes required for growth and shift from a people-based structure to a function-based structure. The momentum continued to build as he empowered his head of HR to formalize roles and responsibilities with employee input, promoted the senior nurse to a pivotal senior management role in the medical care part of the business, and hired a head of sales so the leads that were previously coming to him could be acted on without delay, since he did not have the time to follow up promptly.

We worked together to restructure the company, empowering key staff and freeing up his time so he could think about strategic acquisitions, seek out new value-added partners, and dedicate time to developing client segment growth plans. The action my client took in Pillar I to invest in himself, to create a "better him," served as a key spark, enabling him to start putting the plans for the growth that he so keenly desired in place. I share this with you to reinforce the power of Pillar I—investing in yourself is always the best return on investment.

Now that you, too, are better at managing you, let's proceed to being a better manager, which is the second pillar of the Elite Performance Pillars™.

CAN YOU SEE THE REAL ME?

The song "The Real Me" was written by Pete Townshend and appeared on The Who's *Quadrophenia* album in 1973. It concerns a boy named Jimmy and describes how he angrily deals with several individuals to prove that they do not see the real him.

I saw this song's story played out in the workplace so many times in my career in the form of someone knocking on my office door and informing me that they were about to leave the firm. The pent-up frustration had built up inside this individual because, just like The Who's fictitious Jimmy, they were distraught we couldn't see the "real" them. This person would not be a direct report but someone integral to the global sales force. They would explain in that moment of truth that there were many things that they enjoyed in their role at the firm, but there was a certain aspect that had become untenable. It was a cordial, frank discussion. The person had made their mind up and the words exchanged were honest and truthful.

ESTABLISHING THE CORNERSTONE OF DIALOGUE

How can you be a better manager to avoid this recurring pattern of truth that is only discussed when it's too late? It's important to reflect on how you got here so you can become a better manager and prevent this from happening again. How do you get to know the "real me" of staff members before it's too late?

The first step is to get to know your staff members on a personal level and understand their real desires, passions, strengths, and weaknesses. These can be recognized and integrated into their roles and responsibilities to truly achieve the best fit for the individual's motivations and the firm's needs. The key to achieving this is building a different type of dialogue. You must begin with the employee, allowing them to express their strengths, passions, and weaknesses to try to understand their "real me." This step is often overlooked or not given enough importance. But to be an elite manager, you must establish an honest dialogue from the outset.

The important next step is to ask the employees about themselves and then practice active listening. Genuine communication is key to empowering your employees. Share your own strengths, passions, and weaknesses to build trust, opening the channel of communication and allowing them to share their story with you. If you do not ask, if you do not make this attempt to get to know the employee, you will never know what the employee is thinking, their aspirations and passions, or who they really are until it is too late. Changing the dialogue in this way also increases the employee's ownership of their own actions (contributions versus being told). You give them the opportunity to tell you about themselves, their strengths, and areas of development.

Let's go back in time to before the employee came into my office. This scene is so often repeated. You as a manager expect the employee to perform a range of tasks. The person may be an excellent salesperson, an extrovert who is willing to engage, able to help bring in new clients, and very committed to the firm. However, you need the employee to also execute operational functions and follow up on specific administrative tasks to complete the value chain of your business.

Let's say you take the tried-and-true approach of providing the person with autonomy to complete the task and just ask to be updated on the progress. You are pleased that you are not micromanaging the situation, and you truly hope that the person will simply apply themself to the task and keep you updated along the way. However, the employee becomes frustrated, since they loathe the tedious operational task, and this frustration starts to cast a shadow on you as their manager and on the job itself.

This was the situation one of my clients faced as an executive at a small software company. They had a senior salesperson who was excellent with clients. He played a key role in getting the company off the ground, but unfortunately, he wasn't as proficient on the operational side or at following up. This is a common challenge for many businesses, especially startups. To make the matter even more complicated, this senior salesperson was my client's best man at his wedding. My client wanted the best for the salesperson, his close personal friend, but the business relationship was becoming untenable. As my client delegated project work to the senior salesperson, he expected regular updates and progress reports. However, weeks went by with no communication, and frustration began to mount. Despite valuing the salesperson's skills and having a close personal relationship, my client was disappointed and dismayed that administrative tasks were being neglected. How could this downward spiral be reversed to de-stress the situation for both my client and the salesperson involved?

CREATE A SAFE ENVIRONMENT TO BUILD HONEST DIALOGUE

I coached my client through the steps discussed above in Pillar II: make the employee feel safe; have an honest discussion; and listen to the employee express their desires, passions, and areas of weakness. You as a manager can significantly influence the situation if you put the person at ease and genuinely tell them that you want to know, for the good and welfare of the firm, where they believe they can best contribute and areas that are not their strengths. In this situation, my client found an appropriate time to have the discussion, and both parties were glad they found the opportunity to deal with the elephant in the room. My client wanted to promote his friend, whom he trusted to be his right-hand man, his chief operating officer. Meanwhile, the salesperson did not want to disappoint his friend, so he tried to go along, even though he just wanted to focus on sales. The salesperson was content to continue as a senior salesperson and was okay if my client hired someone to be the COO.

Working with your employees, your N-1s, is perhaps one of the more complex dynamics in the workplace. Ironically, I have found that the closer you are personally with someone, or even if you are just friendly or social acquaintances outside work, the more difficult it can sometimes be to have the formality of a manager-employee relationship.

During the early stages of my career, I remember being caught up in the idea that everyone in the workplace shared my same work ethic and approach. It seemed logical to me that, at the end of the day, one could assume that people would be like-minded about how they performed their jobs—be it finance, professional athletics, or other lucrative careers—because the reward was significant. Looking back, I realize how naive that belief was. The reality is that not everyone operates the same way and not everyone has the same level of tenacity. It's important to approach each individual as their own unique person rather than thinking they will all fit into a certain mold.

Unless your employees feel safe and you create an environment where they can be honest, they may simply mimic what you want to see instead, reinforcing your assumption that they are like-minded. But the lack of honest dialogue simply casts a veil on the reality. To prevent the false understanding or false sense of security that everyone is like you, that they see things as clearly as you do and implicitly understand the execution of the mission as you do, you must change the basis of your interaction. A better manager seeks to ensure mutual clarity on roles and expectations, thus minimizing discrepancies in expectations.

FOUR COMPONENTS OF ACTIVE LISTENING

To be a better manager and create a high-performing team, you must be both an effective and decisive communicator and an active listener. I have found that the following four techniques make active listening most successful: being fully present in the conversation by listening without making judgments or taking a position on an issue, allowing the speaker to finish thoughts without interruption, asking open-ended questions to clarify information and encourage further discussion, and summarizing what you heard to ensure you understand the speaker's message. As a manager, be an active listener, take the time up front to ensure roles and expectations are clear, and then continue this down the chain of command.

One thing that I have found to be essential when building strong and meaningful relationships with employees is to create an environment in which they feel comfortable and safe to talk about their passions and challenges. In my experience, a good way to start the conversation is by acknowledging that there's a lot of work to be done and that everyone has a key role to play. I usually say something like, "We have a lot of things coming up and our workload is going to increase. It's important that we all execute our tasks to the best of our abilities. I want to know what you're best at and what you find more challenging. That way, we can make sure you're working on deliverables that play to your strengths." By taking this approach, I've been able to have some really valuable conversations with my team and help them excel in their roles.

Let the person answer the question. The critical part of the exercise is to pause and truly let the employee respond, thereby cultivating a positive and productive work environment. Let them tell you how they feel and what they believe are their strengths and weaknesses in their own words. The setup is vital. It must be an authentic and penalty-free environment. It can also help if you share your own strengths and weaknesses as an icebreaker. Ideally, you can create a symbiotic tenet, a relationship between their personal values and the responsibilities and deliverables they have within the organization. Why is this so important? First, if you are successful in creating an authentic environment where people can speak freely, you may be surprised at what the employees say. What they reveal and share can be instrumental in really aligning and reducing frustration between the employee and manager. Similarly, identifying someone's strengths and weaknesses in the first person is very powerful because you will also see their level of self-awareness.

The key is establishing trust in the discussion so that the person is not guarded. Create a situation that's penalty-free. That is the magic of honest and candid dialogue, which is what you're seeking to accomplish. If you care for others and are kind, people feel that and will give it back in return.

The same technique of letting the employee have the "pen" and speak candidly should be applied to the formal HR task of defining one's roles and responsibilities (as discussed earlier, an example is how my health care client implemented this at his company). For me, the employee must categorically have written roles and responsibilities. Give them the pen to make edits or acknowledge that the representation accurately reflects what the person does.

Ask the employee if it is comprehensive. If not, you will want to update the roles and responsibilities as the firm changes so they clearly reflect what the person does and what the organization counts on them doing each day. In the implementation of the documented roles and responsibilities, HR and management will have the final pen, but only after the employee has been sincerely given the opportunity to contribute. Did they take the exercise seriously and reflect on how they spend their time? Identifying things that the employee does that their manager is just unaware of should be a healthy and constructive exercise.

The power of this exercise is that you hear directly from the employees about their roles and responsibilities. Getting their firsthand perspective helps you as a manager understand what is working well and what could be improved. It also shows that you value their input and want to make sure everyone is set up for success.

The next step is reviewing this understanding. Then, you as the manager round it out and correct it. Give that feedback to the employee (even if it's an "as is") so you have aligned roles and responsibilities. By providing employees with the opportunity to contribute to the definition of their roles and responsibilities, this initiative enables them to gain a sense of empowerment, which in turn fosters ownership and accountability. This approach ensures that everyone is on the same page and working toward the same goals. If you dictate one way without feedback, there can be resentment or just misalignment.

Giving them the opportunity to define what they do can make you aware of unsung heroic aspects (work they do that is not known or recognized). Likewise, you can better appreciate where they are focused and ensure your communicated mission intent is clearly understood by the employee. Now that you have a foundation, and the employee has defined and taken ownership of what they do, you will review it to ensure that the definition is aligned with the goals and priorities of the firm and move forward.

The same process should be used for mid-year and year-end reviews. I always found it most helpful for the employee to provide a draft. This is informative because it will quickly tell you how self-aware they are. Why is this important? Again, having ownership—the employee's level of accountability when given the opportunity to tell you about what they succeeded in and their strengths and weaknesses (which, I think, is always fair)—allows the employee to paint their picture instead of you painting the picture first and then getting their feedback.

Also, I was always surprised at the wide range of preparedness exhibited by individuals regarding their self-evaluations. Some employees would be comprehensive, taking that extra step and thinking about how they could provide a draft that thoroughly reflected their best efforts in their voice or tone on your behalf. I was not too concerned if it was boastful. I focused on how seriously they applied themselves to the exercise. For example, thoughtful employees would anticipate that employee reviews today need to have quantitative content (as some reviews may be subject to regulatory review). Other employees would anticipate that perhaps the electronic submission form would only accept a certain number of words and try to anticipate what requirements the manager would face in completing the appraisal (statements supported by facts, figures, and trends and the appropriate length required for the exercise if known ahead of time).

Additionally, you'll quickly see whether they understand the items of the team's mission that are critical for you. Maybe the absence of certain things is both a statement about the employee being tuned in with your mission but also a reflection on you. If that employee omits something you see as critical to your mantra, is your guidance on what is important clear and concise? Do you successfully instill the key one to three deliverables in your employees? If you were to plot a histogram, what would the distribution look like regarding the core objectives for your group? If as a manager you have a simple, focused core message that consistently repeats, emphasizing banging the drum on the two to three key objectives, the histogram should be a tight distribution. However, if there's a wide distribution, the sender isn't delivering the central objectives in a way that is broadly understood.

THE TEAM'S EFFICIENCY IS EQUIVALENT TO THE CLARITY OF THE COMMANDER'S INTENT

The commander's intent is the commander's expression of the mission's purpose, which should be broad enough to allow for initiative and flexibility by subordinates while staying aligned with the higher commander's goals (we'll discuss this in detail in Chapter 9).

Stop! This is important. If your team doesn't have a highly correlated understanding of your key objectives, you have a problem. Think about this: If you study military history, you will know the ideas of mass and momentum from Carl von Clausewitz's *Principles of War*. If you are not familiar with his principles, the message is that you will be less efficient when the efforts of the group are inherently diluted. If you're not a military buff, don't fret. Allow me to illustrate how some of the principles used in the military can be incredibly useful in the workplace. As someone with a military background, I can attest that these principles are effective in organizing and guiding individuals toward a shared objective. While the stakes may be higher in the military, the fundamental principles are still applicable in any workplace setting.

Carl von Clausewitz was a Prussian general and military theorist who wrote *Principles of War* in 1812, which has been republished many times. His writings retain remarkable contemporary merit and relevance in explaining the critical elements affecting warfare in the modern era. According to Clausewitz, military commanders must apply unrelenting pressure and energy to defeat the enemy. Military commanders must amass combat power against the enemy's vulnerability, creating or revealing additional weaknesses that the attacking force can exploit. In other words, commanders must capitalize on speed, surprise, and shock to destroy the enemy.[14]

The key lesson for elite managers is that if your staff does not have a clear understanding of the "commander's intent" (one of the ten tenets of being an exceptional manager discussed in detail below), their day-to-day work efforts will have built-in slippage. They will spend time and effort with good intent on things that are not aligned with their core objectives.

One key to success is to amplify your areas of responsibility, initiatives, and contributions. You must have a consistent mantra, such that everyone on the team knows it and incorporates it into their day-to-day.

---

14 Von Clausewitz, Carl. *Principles of War*. Courier Corporation, 2012.

Develop a simple mantra with no more than three key points. Beat this like a drum. Promote it and have fun with it, but demand that the exertion and focus of effort be weighed against the mantra in all actions, presentations, et cetera. In the mantra, you must set the tone. Define your principles for the team, the immutable truths that are the foundation for the team, and help guide management through those principles. The benefit here as a manager, if you're doing the job purposefully, is that every interaction between your direct manager or others in the firm and your team will, at least in part, reflect your mantra, so the impression becomes the reality. It sounds to others that your team has a clear mission, a unified purpose, a common bond, and unequivocal understanding. If you choose the mission correctly, your boss will see that the message comes through and your team is truly aligned with what's important to the firm.

When your messaging is simple and clear, it can have a powerful impact on your team. Your direct reports will have a better understanding of your goals and priorities, and they can communicate that clarity to others. When your managers and other stakeholders openly discuss options in light of your objectives, it can become the best brand advertising you can design. This creates a ripple effect that can benefit your organization in many ways.

Now your group has an identity, both up and down in the organization. Employees know what is important in the big picture. Your management will perceive a focused, intentional group of people all pursuing the same goal—not because you tell them this but because they see and hear it in their own observations and interactions.

In summary, Being a Better Manager has three components:

1. Let your employees have the pen. It's imperative that your N-1s have the pen to give them the opportunity to share (if you can make them feel safe to do so) what they enjoy in the job, the areas where they do not think they excel, and the areas where perhaps someone else would be better off executing this part of the mission. The goal is to enable them to see themselves as others see them. In other words, giving them the pen or microphone helps raise their self-awareness so they can raise their self-mastery.

2. Choose a management mantra to ensure that your employees have clarity of purpose. The mantra should consist of the two or three things, stated succinctly, that are mission critical to you, which should be inexplicably linked to your management's priorities (we'll discuss this further in the upcoming chapters). Now you have a force multiplier in that everyone in your team is consistent about what you're trying to do and what's important, so the voice will be the same. Efficiency and effectiveness will be laser-focused and will take on a ripple effect across the organization and out to your clients.

3a. As a team leader, it's important to make time for your employees to be open and honest with you. Let them know that they are valued and essential members of the team, but also acknowledge when there are areas where they may not excel or may struggle to deliver on mission-critical tasks. By doing so, you help them gain greater self-awareness and insight into their strengths and weaknesses. Continual alignment is key to building a strong, transparent, and effective team. You want to make sure that when changes come in the organization (although never easy), they understand that they were asked, they gave their feedback, and that if the roles were reversed (if they were the recipient of the feedback), they could comprehend the changes that may follow. Learn how to motivate and inspire team members by getting to know each employee well. Utilize the symbiotic tenet (as a reminder, I recently introduced this concept as part of the four components of active listening) such that you as a manager connect the team's mission and related objectives to the employee's values.

3b. One-on-ones should not feel like an unnecessary administrative task for the employee. You need to change the construct if this is the case. An integral part of being a better manager is to reposition this interaction so you take on the role of their coach. In this coaching capacity, your modus operandi is to provide your support and guidance to help them succeed. Show genuine care and consciously make the meeting about them so they will open up so you can help them succeed. It is important to have a structured but simple template so that, as their manager, you can convey that your main focus is to provide them with assistance and support wherever necessary. However, in order for you to gain a clear understanding of the status of their projects, you need the information provided in a well-organized, structured way that's easy to comprehend. I have found that an effective technique is asking the employee a question such as, "Would you be able to provide me with an honest progress report regarding the current state of affairs, including any noteworthy successes and challenges that require attention? This will enable me to better understand how I can assist you in achieving our shared objectives." This helps remove the appearance of being an administrative task by keeping it simple and focused on how you can help them. Simple is powerful, because when the content can literally be bullet points written down on a mobile device, no one has an excuse. If we stick to the three to five FAST objectives, producing the content should be an efficient process and represent their day-to-day focus as far as the salient points of the key objectives and where they stand.

A word on feedback in this process: this is an area that most of us, even seasoned, top-performing managers, continually need to work on. First, always deliver any negative feedback in private, behind closed doors. In the heat of the moment, delivering public, negative feedback can be very detrimental to both the employee and to you as the manager. When giving feedback, use the time for your scheduled one-on-ones (block out these times and choose a frequency that is manageable—biweekly is suggested.)

Another technique that I've found to be successful is instead of telling people what to do, I provide personal viewpoints to help guide them to make the best decisions. I shared the following simple example many times in my career with salespeople who worked for me.

Know one thing for sure: when you are speaking with a client, there is absolutely no one else in the world speaking with your client at that particular time. It's just you and them. Think about that as a competitive barrier to entry and how valuable every opportunity to speak with a client is, as it is truly unique and powerful. This motivates me to make the calls and engage with clients because, in each discussion, I have a unique opportunity to add value to the relationship. I would encourage the salesperson to practice *carpe diem*—seize the day. I shared this perspective to encourage the salesperson to make the most of the present, make that call, and take full advantage of the opportunity in front of them today, rather than worrying about the future. In a similar vein, I would share my tactic to swim upstream and challenge myself to call on difficult clients who had the means to conduct business. It was simply a matter of tenacity, knowing that the client had to do business with someone. I would aim to simply persevere for the long term and outlast other salespeople who may be tempted to give up. This simple exchange of viewpoints helped break the ice and let them know that I had faced challenges in my day and found simple ways to motivate myself.

CHAPTER 8 TAKEAWAYS

- Being the best "you" allows you to be a better manager.

- Create a safe environment in which you can build honest dialogue with your employees.

- To be a better manager and create a high-performing team, you must be both an effective and decisive communicator and an active listener.

- Your staff must have a clear understanding of the "commander's intent."

TEN CORE TENETS OF AN ELITE MANAGER

"A manager is a guide. He takes a group of people and says, 'With you, I can make us a success; I can show you the way.'"

—ARSENE WENGER

BEING A BETTER manager requires you to communicate well, but why? Oftentimes, managers make assumptions and expect what they want to accomplish to be implicit. The result is a chain reaction of inefficiency. The team is distracted and expends valuable time and energy on what they think the managers want to accomplish. Within the team, this unintended ambiguity in the delivery of the team's mission can erode the very circle of respect and trust that managers have tried so hard to create. In turn, the manager gets frustrated because they do not see the team focusing on what they think is important. Furthermore, teams get frustrated because they learn that what they have been working on is not what management wants. All of these symptoms are usually the result of managers not communicating well.

In the business world, poor communication can lead to inefficiency as described above, including loss of revenue, failed projects, poor morale, and poor execution. If you want to raise the stakes and seek out an environment where the consequences of poor communication are much higher, the military provides an excellent environment to learn from. The correlation between the efficiency of the communication and the task continues to rise as the stakes increase. The military provides one of the best references for effective management communication. On today's integrated, digital battlefield, communication must be precise and clear. When lives are at stake, you simply cannot have imperfect communication because the consequences can result in casualties. The military has a ready guide that all managers can adopt; it meets the stringent requirements of the battlefield, but can be applied in the business world with outstanding effectiveness.

CORE TENET 1: BE THE COMMANDER AND STATE YOUR INTENT

"Commander's intent" is a military term that I ask each of my executive coaching clients, as well as you as an elite performer, to adopt. In the military, the commander's intent is the commander's personal expression of the purpose of the operation—a broad description and definition of what a successful mission will look like that allows subordinates to exercise judgment and initiative, and depart from the original plan when the unforeseen occurs, in a way that is consistent with the higher commander's aims. It consists of three elements: (1) why—the purpose, (2) how—the method of execution, and (3) goal—the desired end state of the battlefield. For military operations, we typically frame the end state from the perspective of friendly forces or "customers," enemy forces or "competitors," and the environment or "market."

Let's look at a battlefield example of commander's intent. According to an article by Harvard Business Review, "During World War II, the sea and airborne invasion of France on June 6, 1944, (D-day) had been planned for years. British, Canadian, and American airborne forces planned and rehearsed a precise series of glider and parachute landings that were designed to secure bridges, road junctions, and other key terrain that would enable the ground invasion forces to advance rapidly inland. The airborne invasion forces took off from England and months of planning appeared to vanish instantly. Parachute forces dropped into unmarked landing zones, gliders landed in the wrong areas, and thousands of soldiers from different units were mixed together in the night. It appeared that a military disaster had occurred. Yet, only hours later, the original military objectives were [being] accomplished by ad-hoc units that faced much fiercer German resistance. Commander's Intent had saved the day. Leaders and soldiers at all levels understood that no matter where they landed, they had to form into units and seize the bridges and key terrain. The plan was a failure, but good Commander's Intent and superior training allowed improvisation and initiative to save the mission."[15]

As a manager in the business world, your communication of the mission at the start of each year, updated as circumstances require, necessitates a leader's mindset. You are the commander and must state your clear intent on the corporate battlefield. Your communication is critical to the performance of your team and, ultimately, your performance as a leader. The litmus test determines if the quality of your communication has prepared your team and stakeholders to execute your intent. If your employees face chaos on the corporate battlefield, can they reconstitute, improvise, and achieve your desired end state?

To help you, I have prepared a checklist to ensure that your team communication as a manager meets the criteria.

---

15   Chad Storlie, "Manage Uncertainty with Commander's Intent," Harvard Business Review, November 3, 2010, https://hbr.org/2010/11/dont-play-golf-in-a-football-g.

- Clearly address the *why* and the *how* upfront.
- Ensure the goal is well defined from the vantage point of the customer vis-à-vis competitors and your firm's desired position in the market.
- Establish a single mantra that is the unifying focus for your team. It must be well-understood by all members and the key support functions.
- Communicate your vision clearly. The best managers know what's important and make sure all team members understand the mission so the team can adapt to the changing business environment and still deliver on their desired end state.

If done correctly, the empowering part will be that your communication encourages people to take initiative toward your intent, the desired end state. The momentum will start to build as you ensure that there is a clear understanding of your intent at each level in the chain of command (in the corporate world, this is equivalent to the management organization chart).

The key to business success as a manager is putting your team first. Equip them so they know your desired end state. You have the responsibility of clearly communicating. If you raise your individual bar such that you hold yourself accountable to the highest standard using the commander's intent checklist, you have completed the first step. Start with the employee and reverse the traditional model. Review your intent—the mission for the team—with the employee to ensure there is clear understanding. Then, ask the employee to express their strengths, passions, and weaknesses with respect to their understanding of the mission and how they would seek to accomplish it.

ORGANIC EXCELLENCE:
PUTTING PIECES OF THE PUZZLE TOGETHER

This is a profound change from traditional management where the objectives are dictated by the manager to the employee. Your role as a better manager is to be clear with your intent and, after verifying their understanding of your desired end state, to ask the employee to explain how they can best contribute to achieving your intent in their current role. The role of the manager has now changed—you need to fit the pieces of the puzzle together to try to best align people's inherent strengths and weaknesses to the overall execution of the mission.

In the military, you have to achieve peak performance with the organic team you have. You do not have access to a headhunter to recruit or hire others. You have the team you are given, and you must make the most of the people you have. We covered this earlier. Your role as a leader is to inspire and make the effort to get to know each employee well. One effective way to improve the work dynamic between managers and employees is to build strong relationships with team members. Opening communication channels means adopting both the techniques of communicating clear intent and encouraging employees to voice their thoughts and ideas. This approach allows managers to create a more collaborative, symbiotic work environment and to set FAST objectives together.

In every case, I believe the manager needs to stretch themselves, utilize the reverse inquiry FAST goal-setting technique, and take on the embedded challenge of making the most of the team they have. As a reminder, the reverse inquiry technique starts with allowing the employee to express how they are best suited to accomplish your intent and then utilizes the frequently reviewed, ambitious, specific, and transparent goal-setting technique (courtesy of our friends at MIT.)

Each military leader accepts this challenge, and I encourage you to adopt the same mindset and strive to achieve organic excellence whenever possible.

CORE TENET 2: SOLVE THE PUZZLE—BE A CONDUCTOR (KNOW THEIR CORE COMPETENCIES)

The critical success factor for the puzzle solver, the elite manager, is knowing the capacity of the team by knowing the core competencies of each individual—what motivates them, what drives them, and what really makes them tick on the inside. If you understand this, you have solved the puzzle and made yourself a conductor. The intrinsic benefit is that you have simultaneously taken the steps to create an elite team by starting with your team members and the mission and its pending success tailored to their self-expressed capabilities.

Aligning the tasks and objectives with the individual's strengths prompts a metamorphosis for the manager in which they become a better manager, an elite performer, since this creates natural momentum and positive kinetic energy. Again, by establishing trust and creating a safe environment, you have direct input from team members on where they would like to lean in and the areas that are not their strongest. Not everyone is going to have objectives that perfectly match their combined strengths and weaknesses, but by going through this process, you truly put the employees first and take the steps to create a virtuous circle of trust. It is crucial for the team's overall success in executing the mission that your desired end state is clearly expressed in your commander's intent statement. This will ensure that everyone understands the overall objective and can work toward achieving it together.

CORE TENET 3: FIRST ASK, THEN ACTIVELY LISTEN

If you are going to be a better manager, you need better engagement. I am pounding the table here because too few managers ever really engage with their direct reports. Instead of dictating top down, you need to reverse that pattern and prioritize establishing meaningful dialogue. This is the pull mentality of the Push and Pull Rule (we will discuss push and pull in full detail in the upcoming chapters on Pillar III: Managing Your Manager).

The urgent action here is that you must first ask the employee what responsibilities they would ideally like to have and why. The important difference here is that you are starting from the employee, as we discussed earlier. Give them the pen or the microphone rather than assuming that you know what they want to do. This is the game changer in being an elite manager—to first ask the employee and then actively listen. My mind tends to race ahead, so if you are like me, it will take practice and self-discipline to build your active listening skills. Keep the image of the puzzle solver in your mind—your end state is the picture of the finished puzzle on the cover of the box. Your job is to figure out how all of the pieces (the employees on your team) fit together to achieve the desired end state.

You need to listen attentively to best understand how this person fits in the puzzle and what they can bring to bear in the process. Along the way, you'll need to ask clarifying questions, reflect back through their answers to validate the fit, and confirm that you understood them via positive affirmation through body language. Instead of the typical interaction where you spend most of the time telling, if you've clearly explained the commander's intent, you'll be incentivized to understand how this specific person believes they can contribute to the success of the mission. As you get to know each valuable piece (employee) of the puzzle better, you will become much better at putting the pieces together by building more effective relationships with your team members, internal stakeholders, and clients, but only if you ask first and then actively listen.

CORE TENET 4: ALIGN OBJECTIVES WITH PERSONAL VALUES (SYMBIOSIS)

The best way to motivate people is to create a context where they are self-motivated. To achieve this as a manager, you need to invest the time in getting to know your direct reports well. To be clear, there is a difference between getting to know direct reports and forming friendships. Knowledge does not imply friendship, but it does necessitate making the effort to get to know the team member on a more personal basis. I am asking you to dedicate the time to focus on them; be authentic; and ask them what their passions are, what is important to them, and where they think they can best contribute and why.

Another valuable lesson I learned from working with my health care executive client was that you can realize some unforeseen benefits by systematically reaching out to employees to allow them to voice the areas where they feel they can best contribute and share their aspirations. During the exercise at the health care firm, we also incorporated work-life balance questions designed for the post-COVID-19 era. In coordination with the newly appointed head of HR, we asked what employees' ideal work-life situations would look like and what they would be willing to give back to the firm in exchange for their ideal work situation to make it fair for both parties. The unforeseen benefits he realized were as follows: Some employees expressed the desire to have more flexible work hours after their children's school let out but were willing to provide evening coverage after dinner, which met a critical need for the firm. Others expressed a sincere desire to take on more responsibility to help solidify the management structure and assist in the executive's stated objective to grow revenues by ten times in five years. Still others shared that they were content with their current role and compensation, providing upward mobility opportunities for others keen to progress in their careers.

The bottom line is that the return on investment for spending time with your team members is significant. Carving this time out to be an active listener will enable you to gain an insightful understanding of what drives your individual team members. Your job is to have a clear understanding of the desired end state of the mission and then best determine how you can assign specific team members to tasks that are aligned with their values and passions.

Mastering this skill will give you operational leverage. In the golden decade of my career, I fully embraced the team member dialogue we have been discussing. As a team, we became more efficient. This was in part because I held myself to a heightened standard, ensuring that, as a corporate commander, my intent was clearly understood. I also became an accomplished puzzle solver, one who could put the right team members in the right places (like the pieces of a puzzle) to execute the mission because I had invested the time in getting to know them on a more personal level. The gains in efficiency allowed me to focus more time on mastering the Elite Performance Pillars™, investing in myself, and then mastering the techniques in Pillar II to make me a better manager.

If you can successfully knit the FAST objectives together with the specific people whose expressed motivations, values, and passions match the task, you have achieved one of the most important jobs of a manager. Take the time to assess the critical tasks and assign the pieces of the puzzle to the employees with the best symbiotic fit. If correctly done, the metamorphosis that occurs will change you from a manager to a coach, especially if you can accomplish the symbiotic fit on an individual basis across your entire team. Now, you have created a synergistic environment where the motivation to achieve the task comes from within the individual. As an elite manager/coach, you interact in a more impactful manner by helping, advising, and supporting the process, but the inertia of self-motivation from within the individual team members is the powerful force of unleashed kinetic energy that drives the team forward to accomplish the mission.

Invest your management time in getting to know your people and you will be on your way to creating a team of elite performers. With interests better aligned, team members will have bought into the task, so you will not expend excess energy on convincing or pushing them to focus on the mission. Instead, employees will be self-motivated, and you can then develop an enhanced manager-team member relationship in which you achieve something that is important to them but also important to you. This newly formed relationship enables you to take on the role of a coach. Likewise, team members can gain a different appreciation of your contributions rather than seeing you as just a taskmaster. They can learn from the insights that you share with them and have a greater appreciation of what value you bring to the team by tapping into your skill set to help them succeed in their roles, creating a win-win relationship.

CORE TENET 5: COACH, DON'T TELL

As an experienced manager, your reaction might be, "I already do this." But I want to push this a bit further because, at our level of proficiency, I believe it is a game of finesse. Small, subtle improvements to your personal management tool kit, practiced over time, can have significantly positive results. Let's go back to the golf course, when I was reinforcing bad habits on the driving range. My intentions—to improve my drive by going to the range—were good, but the result did not help me progress my game to the next level. So, I booked a session with a golf coach to help improve my swing. He had a calming demeanor. After warming up, the first thing he said was, "Let me see you hit a couple with your seven iron."

This was an important reminder to me that oftentimes, with good intent, a manager's first inclination is to tell the employee what to do instead of asking them to describe how they are currently approaching the task. Going back to the previous tenet, you already have insight into how the puzzle piece fits into the team's mission—what motivates this person. Couple this knowledge with active listening and resist the inherent reaction to tell first. Instead, assist the person by helping them learn an improved process or technique. Have them play it back to see if they understand the potential benefits of what you are helping them to learn. Asking them what they have tried, exactly where they are stuck, and making suggestions to help them change their approach to resolving the issue and their perspective of the pain points enhances their problem-solving capabilities.

As a coach, you are trying to give them tools, demonstrate how the tools work, and let them practice with the tools to learn and grow through experience, but all the while they are investing in their own personal tool kit. Help them visualize the situation from different perspectives, making them aware of the range of possibilities, and encourage them to explore different avenues—to hover above it, if you will, and view it through a different prism, instead of just in a linear fashion, to help illuminate other options to consider.

Coaching as a manager is an interactive process that involves positive reinforcement and supporting employees' efforts with feedback and guidance to help them improve their performance. Sir John Whitmore, a leading figure in executive coaching, defines coaching as "unlocking a person's potential to maximize their own performance. It is helping them to learn rather than teaching them."[16]

CORE TENET 6: CELEBRATE THE SMALL WINS

Simple things go a long way. One of my favorite clients at a major institution used to always say, "Let's get some small wins and then we can celebrate." We went through a long and arduous process to bring together two large firms with different cultures, but we knew the value exchange between the firms could be in the hundreds of millions of dollars if we were steadfast. Boy, did it feel good in the early years to celebrate some of the small wins together. It gave both firms the encouragement to keep at it and find the next win. Building on our success, the wins became bigger and bigger, but it all started by celebrating the small wins. Recognizing small wins and acknowledging hard work goes a long way with team members. It doesn't cost anything, and if you want a high-performing team, they need your support and praise. The difficult days will come again, but this simple acknowledgment that you provide will give them the encouragement they need on those days to find the next small win they can accomplish, because they know it will be recognized.

---

16 Whitmore, John. *Coaching for Performance*. Nicholas Brealy Publishing, 2009.

CORE TENET 7: MISSION STRONG (ALIGN THE MISSION TO THEIR STRENGTHS)

Investing time in truly getting to know your team members dramatically improves your probability of success. Instead of assigning tasks to be done, align the team member's role in accomplishing the team's goal with their internal values and passions. The best managers are puzzle solvers who carefully match tasks with individuals' strengths and motivations.

CORE TENET 8: BEGIN WITH THE END IN MIND

Stephen R. Covey once wrote, "To begin with the end in mind means to start with a clear understanding of your destination. It means to know where you're going so that you better understand where you are now and so that the steps you take are always in the right direction."[17]

If you want to be elite, you must be able to commit. Put a stake in the ground and be unequivocally exact about what your team will accomplish. Be audacious and commit to goals that are a stretch and that might draw critics but are plausible, that is, ones where everyone is convinced that you are convinced. It's time to aim high and push yourself to the limit. With hard work, determination, and a positive attitude, you can accomplish anything you set your mind to. Remember, the only limitations are those we impose on ourselves. If you are not ambitious, you should not be in the role.

People want to come to work with a purpose. They want to belong to something, to be part of a binding force that unifies collective efforts. To begin with the end in mind empowers everyone. It's a shared vision that will naturally lend

---

17 Covey, Stephen R. *The 7 Habits of Highly Effective People: Powerful Lessons in Personal Change.* Free Press, 2004.

itself to increased collaboration and a collegial spirit. As a leader, you need to openly share and collaborate with people regarding why they are doing what they are doing and reinforce this frequently. Publicly stating your team's mission is an integral part of building your brand. This builds an identity both internally for team members and externally regarding what your team stands for and seeks to achieve. If there is a void, or an unanswered destination in the workplace, this causes stress. Our brains are wired in such a way that the work we do has to have an end purpose. If not, it is disturbing to our brains. Skepticism and doubt creep in, and the efficiency of the team will be impacted. Having a common purpose and a shared goal galvanizes efforts. It fills this uncomfortable void that exists without a clear statement of intent.

During my time at Cambridge University, I experienced an unsettling incident in one of my MBA classes. The professor did not show up, leaving us with a void where he would have usually stood and lectured. Instead, there was a man standing in the back corner of the room who didn't introduce himself or explain what was going on. We had no idea who he was or why he was there. The level of anxiety rose quickly, and agitation filled the room in minutes. The absence of purpose was quite disturbing to us all. I personally felt that if there was no stated purpose for being there, I had better things to do. Some of my classmates stayed, while others, like me, left. However, this lack of purpose impacted us all in different ways. Later, we learned that it was an experiment, and the next time the class was held with the professor present, we discussed how we felt. Many people shared that they felt a very high level of anxiety as there was an unexpected void with no explanation for it. Others, like me, were frustrated, as we arrived on time with the expectation of receiving a lecture. If this much anxiety can be created in such a short period of time, just imagine how your team can be impacted if you don't share with them the end goal at the beginning.

CORE TENET 9: BE CHURCHILL—BE PREPARED. BE MEMORABLE.

Each time you are given an opportunity to be in the spotlight, you must own it. Every opportunity you are given to present at a town hall, speak at an offsite meeting, kick off a client event, or give a talk at any industry event, you must be at your best. This goes back to owning everything in your AOR—no excuses.

Being a great speaker requires time for preparation, practice, rewriting, and then practicing again. Winston Churchill was a legendary communicator because he inspired the populous. He gave them hope in their hour of need and was a master of the English language. He knew instinctively how to adapt his speech to his audience and alter his tone depending on the occasion.

You can listen to many of Winston Churchill's key speeches made over his long career on the International Churchill Society website. Take the opportunity to listen to the recordings of his speeches to feel the emotion he could generate using a dramatic pause to create anticipation and his ability to pull his audience in with his powerful voice. What many people don't know is that Churchill was relentless in his preparation. He would spend hours carefully selecting every word of his speeches. He said he would spend an hour working on a single minute of a speech.[18]

---

18 Winston S. Churchill, "An hour [of] Preparation for Each Minute [of] Delivery," Finest Hour, International Churchill Society, September 5, 2013, https://winstonchurchill.org/publications/finest-hour/finest-hour-106/winston-churchill-author-and-historian/.

My favorite Churchill quote is from August 20, 1940: "Never in the field of human conflict was so much owed by so many to so few."[19] The speech came amid German plans for an invasion. He was referring to the ongoing efforts of the Royal Air Force and other Allied aircrew who were fighting in the Battle of Britain, the pivotal air battle with the German Luftwaffe.

So, that is your benchmark. On every occasion in my career when I was given an opportunity to speak or present, I made my preparation the top priority. Set the bar high for yourself and prepare like Churchill to succeed. To help you prepare your presentation, you can refer to my website, *www.ExecPathfinders.com*, to obtain my ten tips for giving a memorable presentation every time.

CORE TENET 10: IN YOU WE TRUST

Creating a situation where employees feel safe is the key to enabling the next level of performance. The next level is where you can excel as a manager because the alignment of the individual's passions and strengths is strong and you as the puzzle master found the right place for this person to fit into the team's mission. For the individual, a new level of job satisfaction is obtained because they are an active participant in the role in which they believe they could best help the team succeed in their mission. The individual now comes to work purposefully, playing on the balls of their feet like an athlete, ready to engage or pivot left or right depending on the needs of the business.

The laws of physics also prevail in the work world. Remember Newton's first law: a body at rest tends to stay at rest unless acted upon by another force. You create trust by

19   History Extra, "8 of Churchill's greatest speeches," *BBC History Magazine*, November 24, 2021, https://www.historyextra.com/period/second-world-war/churchills-greatest-speeches/

opening up to the employee and sharing your vulnerability as a manager in your efforts to best align objectives to their strengths and desires.

The external force added to the equation enables the employee to transform their potential energy into kinetic energy. You have brought energy to the equation by asking the employee what they are truly passionate about. This builds the inertia, or motivation, that will drive them on a daily basis to perform their role. Invest in your team and establish trust and you will transform your role from day-to-day manager to daily coach. It is truly a win-win situation, but only if you can establish trust.

CHAPTER 9 TAKEAWAYS

- Core Tenets to Being a Better Manager:

1. Be the Commander and State Your Intent
2. Solve the Puzzle—Be a Conductor (Know Their Core Competencies)
3. First Ask, then Actively Listen
4. Align Objectives to Personal Values (Symbiosis)
5. Coach, Don't Tell
6. Celebrate the Small Wins
7. Mission Strong (Align the Mission to their Strengths)
8. Begin with the End in Mind
9. Be Churchill—Be Prepared. Be Memorable.
10. In You We Trust

FROM DELEGATION TO PARTNERSHIP

"Trust is the highest form of human motivation."
—STEPHEN COVEY

BUILDING ON CORE tenet ten, "In you we trust" must be the foundation of your relationship with your direct reports if you are going to evolve and be elite. I'll be honest with you; delegation was something I struggled with earlier in my career. After all, managers are accountable for the team's results, but by delegating, they are exposed. This uncomfortable exposure kept me up at night. As a manager, you are working hard to develop your personal brand and be consistent, innovative, and reliable, yet delegation presents an asymmetric risk.

The way I viewed it, through my middle manager lens, was, "Why put the many years dedicated to building my reputation as a manager at risk via delegation?" Although I knew that if I was going to progress, I could not do it all on my own, I still struggled with the traditional idea of delegation. How could I mitigate risk yet share the workload with my direct reports? It was at this point in my management career that I fostered the idea of collaboration, treating the managers who reported to me as partners. By valuing their input and ideas and empowering them to take ownership of their work, we were able to achieve greater success as a team. This idea, coupled with the rule of "ask first, then listen" became powerful.

The steps involved in replacing delegating with partnering included obtaining a better understanding of what my

N-1s wanted to do and what they excelled at doing. Then, the linchpin was trusting them as a partner to determine the *how* of the execution. The technique of partnering actually helped to mitigate risk because the team member and partner felt true ownership in the process. Their own self-esteem and pride drove their internal motivation, attention to detail, and freedom to innovate. However, there had to be an investment up front if the co-ownership of the work and mutual trust were to become binding in purpose. It took work to build these bridges of trust. My goal changed from delegating and managing to the specific goal of spending at least one hour a week with the regional managers to really understand them and what motivated them, as well as practicing asking first, then listening.

The resultant breakthrough was an outcome of sharing my professional vulnerability with direct reports. Collectively, we represented what sales stood for at the bank. It was not personal. It was bigger than any of us as individuals since we were the stewards, the guardians, the bearers of the collective group of 600 sales professionals. As the senior leaders, we collectively stood for sales. What each of us did individually, and what we could do together, formed in the minds of the others.

The change in mindset to one of co-ownership led to joint accountability, far more constructive brainstorming sessions, and people developing a natural affinity for volunteering for tasks that they believed fit their skill set because they were driven by the vision we were building together. As a management team, momentum was built. As the architects, we could shape, mold, and design sales because we shaped the image of the department for senior management through our actions. It was the positioning of what we did collectively that profoundly changed the dynamic for me. It was not me asking the regional managers to perform three to five objectives; rather, it was a mission we collectively shared, and they had three to five objectives they owned as part of the team.

To be a better manager, you must endorse, boldly embrace, and truly believe in why you go to work every day, why you make the sacrifices, and hold yourself accountable to something beyond your yearly performance objectives. You must foster and create that amazing ingredient that is recreated on sports fields around the world when the Cinderella team that does not have a chance on paper, together, with a unified purpose as a team, beats the odds and is victorious. True authentic passion and leading by example (LBE) management styles inspire and engender commitment to the common goal.

I realized that being courageous, being exposed when others realized you were all in without hesitation and that you were steadfastly committed to a goal that you alone could not achieve, is the tipping point when you galvanize the bonds you need to be an elite team. My posture changed. I made a conscious decision to truly lead, set the pace, and guide the team toward success. I knew that their dedication and sense of ownership would be integral to achieving our goals, and I was determined to foster a culture of pride and accountability. Together, we were part of something truly special, and I was honored to lead the way. It was at this point that I realized we could achieve more if I was willing to let go and delegate by partnering. It was full circle. It wasn't about telling my management team the features or the precise result I desired but instead about giving them the context of the problems I was trying to solve and asking them to determine a way to solve the problems and achieve the results. It was about the *how*.

Delegation was the wrong approach, at least in the strict sense. I deleted it from my vocabulary because this was not the technique that would best serve the team. Instead, I developed my management skills to view it as a partnership. I was demanding about what we collectively wanted to achieve, taking an active role and having my oar in the water with the team on key clients and global projects, yet I gave each of my partners the autonomy to execute the *how* because I was authentic in what I aspired us to achieve together. What bound us was this sense of purpose beyond the titles on our business cards. Instead, the onus was on us to determine how global sales as a team would be perceived by observers through our collective actions.

Inherently, achieving this type of genuine buy-in instilled the very pride, attention to detail, and quality control I sought as a reluctant delegator because the flaw was not delegating but unconsciously disallowing people to be part of something, co-designers who jointly owned. It started for me with the interjection of "we" and the elimination of the notion of delegation. Rather, the mission became the collective tasks that we were taking shared ownership of. With this relational transparency, I could be supportive in the process, there to help if needed with the *how* but demanding about what we were trying to achieve because our interests were aligned.

We recognized the weight of responsibility we had toward 600 other professionals, and thus, we challenged ourselves to aspire for excellence and adhere to the highest standards. We understood that not only the staff but their families were depending on us to be rigorous and self-motivated in order to effectively achieve the defined goals and meet the end state of the commander's intent.

If you are following me, it goes back to building Pillar 1: Being a Better You as a foundation. Being a better you allows you to trust yourself and be more exposed, more vulnerable, because this step of faith is based upon the positive expectation you have for your direct reports, whom you have welcomed in to be partners in creating something larger, a collaboration more significant than a linear manager and N-1 relationship.

TRUST EMPOWERS TEAMS

Trust will build. I made it a point to inform my direct reports that I didn't want to micromanage, so it was incumbent upon them to deliver their absolute best efforts. My ask of them was to inform me when they hit roadblocks or were falling behind. I asked for their loyalty in keeping me informed and, in turn, they had autonomy in how to execute. I entrusted them with the standard to uphold. This was the handshake. I counted on their integrity to execute the mission, and, in return, they had pride in what they did because of the implicit trust we established together.

Build trust first. Research has found that teams that trust each other still have disagreements but encounter fewer emotional distractions throughout the process.[20] Moreover, trust does not mean you will always agree but makes it easier to disagree because you respect each other and know that you are trying to achieve the same goal, which can have different solutions.

Add one hour a week with your direct reports to your schedule to build this critical trust and truly get to know the people on your team—your partners. The word *partner* is important. It implies trust and respect for the other. Start

20 Kozlowski, Steve W. J. and Bradford S. Bell. *Work Groups and Teams in Organizations.* John Wiley & Sons, Inc., 2003.

using *partner* in your vocabulary today—it will make you a better manager.

The efficiency you will gain when you establish trust is powerful. Without trust, your brain will worry about endless scenarios, what will happen when you are not there or not copied on the email, as examples. If you have established trust, you will have the utmost confidence that the other person will act in the way you would act and escalate or inform you if necessary. This concept of trust can be expressed as psychological safety.

The same concept applies in sports. There was a study done to examine a team-level conceptualization of achievement goals and the performance outcomes of elite sports teams. The study found that high-performing teams shared two common elements: (1) the team had a shared belief and (2) felt safe to take interpersonal risks. In fact, the dominant factor for outperformance was not complementary skill sets but psychological safety.[21]

At this stage, we've now covered a number of key topics. Please review the handy checklist of the five steps to becoming an elite manager below:

1. Be confident in yourself to trust others.
2. Invest the time to earn their trust.
3. Share the vision of what you will collectively achieve.
4. Let them determine the *how*.
5. Be supportive and demanding, and replace delegation in your tool kit with partnering.

21 Heleen Van Mierlo and Edwin A. J. Van Hooft, "Team Achievement Goals and Sports Team Performance," Sage Publishing, 2020, https://journals.sagepub. com/doi/pdf/10.1177/1046496420913119

As the puzzle solver, working with team members is the priority. Then, you can share the problem you need each of them to solve, aligning the problem with their self-expressed strengths and passions (which you know because you asked first, then actively listened).

THE 40 PERCENT RULE

How many of us really know what we are capable of? Have you ever tested your personal limits or tried to push through the mental wall of what you believed you were incapable of doing? If you have not been in the military, competed at an elite level in sports, or set out to achieve a personal quest (finish your first marathon, complete an Ironman, or execute a class five mountain climb, etc.), you may not know your threshold for discomfort or have a limited belief in your physical or mental ability under duress. As an elite performer, you set the tone. My friend would say, "The speed of the leader is the speed of the pack." Your role now is to be the nucleus of the team, to provide the energy and be courageous. I want to equip each one of you, no matter what your background may be, with the same psychological motivator that Navy SEALs instill in their members. It is called the 40 Percent Rule.

The 40 Percent Rule states that when your mind tells you that you're done, you're really only 40 percent done. You still have 60 percent more in your reserve tank that you can tap into if you have the willpower and determination to do so. You can witness the 40 percent rule in action around the world on a near-weekly basis when amateur runners "hit the wall" in a marathon some point after the ten-mile marker. Some hit it just after, and others hit the wall a few miles later, but in either case, nothing changed with their physical body. It was their mental outlook that changed—that willed them across the finish line. Despite feeling like they could go no further, they did all 26.2 miles. [22]

This is a concept used by Navy SEALs that you can now adapt as an elite manager to increase your mental toughness and push yourself beyond preconceived limits. The good news is that applying the rule does not require you to have prior military training or be a former competitive athlete. It simply requires you to believe and embrace the 40 Percent Rule.

Mental toughness is not just required for physical challenges. It is perhaps even more important when displaying yourself as an elite leader in the workplace. Your mettle as a leader will be formed when the team faces the disappointing news that the beta test of the software failed; or after hours and hours of time spent on the RFP, it did not result in a victory; or a valued client decided to switch to a competitor. This is when you need to be there for encouragement. As you pick yourselves up to continue your steadfast journey as a team to your shared goal, you will need to remind your team members that they have 60 percent more in the reserve tank.

Within your team, you need to identify the members who know they have more in the tank and are willing to push themselves and others. Share a personal story about how you overcame a challenge, and remind them of the 40 Percent Rule as a mental tool they can add to their personal tool kit.

The Navy SEALs use the 40 Percent Rule, but you can choose to be like Mike, instead. Embrace Michael Jordan's perspective: "I've missed more than 9,000 shots in my career. I've lost almost 300 games. Twenty-six times I've been trusted to take the game-winning shot and missed. I've

22 Logan Nye, "The SEAL behind the '40 percent rule' is a fitness beast," We Are the Mighty, October 6, 2022, https://www.wearethemighty.com/mighty-fit/navy-seal-40-percent-rule/.

failed over and over and over again in my life. And that is why I succeed."[23]

To create dynamism in your team, you cannot be the sole source of energy. Pair people up to build new dynamics and further the trust between team members. To be an effective manager in the fast-changing, complex times of today, you have to break out of the traditional management mold of the past. You must be willing to invest the time to break down the walls between professional and human personas. Members of the team will become stronger as you break down the walls and build trust. Offsites and team activities can be a great way to kick-start the process, but it takes effort to sustain a positive work environment. You need to build from the team events and strengthen trust as a core part of your management duties.

The traditional management skills of the past can still be utilized in the day-to-day operation of your business but will not dramatically enhance the overall performance of the team and drive it toward a vision. The time-honored management practices of setting goals, planning, motivating employees, and coaching are all important but not sufficient to be a true manager of change. To be an elite manager today requires a fundamental change in your leadership style. Leading in this context is about changing your mindset to view your direct reports as partners, having the vision of what the team will accomplish for a greater purpose, and letting your partners own the *how* of the execution.

As the puzzle solver, you can see the vision and help guide the pieces (the members of your team) into place. It is the time you have invested in truly getting to know your partners that unlocks the potential of each member.

---

23 Flavia Medrut, "Michael Jordan's Most Powerful Life Lessons for When You Feel Like a Failure," Goalcast, accessed December 6, 2023, https://www.goalcast.com/michael-jordan-life-lessons-on-failure/.

They understand the trust you are extending them because you took the time to hear their professional and personal ambitions, which in turn helped break down the very walls that separated the professional from the personal.

It was a profound transformation in my management career when I decided to switch my leadership style. As an elite manager, transitioning to a more dynamic approach gives you a renewed perspective, allowing you to fully appreciate the numerous advantages that come with organizational change. You now possess the ability to effectively guide your team toward unlocking its full potential. By embracing the 40 percent rule, you can constantly strive to go beyond your perceived limitations. The idea serves as a driving force for your team and instills a sense of energy and motivation in them. Act with unwavering integrity, provide unwavering support, and observe with a smile as your team determines the best methods to achieve your shared vision. As a leader, provide the oxygen to fuel the team's fire by consistently fostering a culture of trust and empowering them to work cohesively and collectively toward your common goal.

Nelson Mandela stated his view on leadership so elegantly: "A leader . . . is like a shepherd. He stays behind the flock, letting the nimblest go out ahead, whereupon the others follow, not realizing that all along they are being directed from behind."[24] It takes courage to let go, to underwrite the risk and to trust your partners in their pursuit of how to execute the vision you have shared. The vision is not about you but something that has a greater purpose and unites you in your collective efforts.

The secret to forming a high-performing team is sharing a vision that your partners take shared ownership of and

24 Mandela, Nelson. *Long Walk to Freedom*. Little Brown & Co., 1994.

are self-motivated to accomplish because they are leveraging their strengths and true passions to do so. Being an elite manager necessitates the application of the Right-Angle Rule of being honest with yourself and the man above such that you know who you are, your strengths and your passions as well as your weaknesses and your dislikes. The personal mastery of this understanding then serves as the foundation of your leadership. As you gain experience as a leader, what are the potential traps you need to avoid?

We have covered Pillar I: Being a Better You and Pillar II: Being a Better Manager, but you will not be an elite performer, achieve all the success you deserve, or experience all the joy you are entitled to unless you master Pillar III: Managing Your Manager. If you want to learn how to master the final critical Elite Performance Pillar™, Pillar III, turn the page to Part IV.

CHAPTER 10 TAKEAWAYS

- The efficiency you will gain when you establish trust with your N-1s is powerful.

- Ask first, then listen to better understand what your N-1s excel at doing. Trust them as partners to determine the how of the execution.

- To be an elite manager today requires a fundamental change in your leadership style. Leading in this context is about changing your mindset to view your direct reports as partners, having a vision of what the team will accomplish for a greater purpose, and trusting your partners to own the how of the execution.

PART IV

PILLAR III: MANAGING YOUR MANAGER

BE AMAZINGLY PREDICTABLE

"Reliability is the precondition for trust."
—WOLFGANG SCHAUBLE

ARLY IN MY CAREER, one of my first managers told me, "This job is as simple or as difficult as you want to make it." There is no better way to encapsulate the relationship you choose to have with your manager. You can have great managers, average managers, and difficult managers, but the rules of managing your manager for elite performers apply to all managers. If you want to be an elite performer, make managing your manager simple and follow these ten conventions.

First, remember your manager is human like you. AI has not taken over yet, so they have good days and bad days, just like you. Like you, they struggle in this world of increasing unknowns, so the premium they place on certainty has never been higher. Therefore, if you want to be greatly valued by your manager, *be amazingly predictable!*

By doing so, you create scarcity value for yourself. When managers get let down by so many things, be amazingly predictable in everything you do that encompasses the top ten rules. Hopefully, for some of you, there's a little light going off and you're flipping through the pages of the book back to Being a Better You.

Guess what? Managing your manager is in your AOR. It relies on conscious actions that you can control. If you want to better manage your manager, commit to taking personal accountability for the ten rules, and I guarantee you will greatly enhance the value that your manager sees in you. Let's get started.

THE TOP TEN RULES OF MANAGING YOUR MANAGER FOR ELITE PERFORMERS

RULE 1: KNOW WHAT IS IMPORTANT

Elite performers know not only what is important to their boss but what is important to *their* bosses, their N+2s. If you make your boss's goals your goals, you will win every time. It's simple—just ask yourself what you can do to help your boss succeed. Start with your personal brand, which should be a compilation of your manager's goals, the goals of the firm, and the Right-Angle Rule. This is where you build exponential momentum.

In practical terms, embrace the following steps:

- **Clearly define your personal brand.** Take the time to identify your unique strengths, passions, and attributes that align with your manager's goals and the firm's objectives. This will help you establish a clear and authentic personal brand.

- **Identify the key pillars of your brand.** Determine core areas of expertise or subject matters that are relevant to your manager's goals or the firm's objectives. These pillars should reflect your skills and strengths, making you the go-to person in those areas. (Remember, key pillars should be aligned with your manager's goals or the firm's goals, so if the firm wants to be number one, part of your brand could be "Clients first in everything we do," embodying how your personal brand intersects with the goals of your manager and the firm in a way that is tailored to your personal and professional attributes.)

- **Continuously develop your knowledge and skills.** Start with demonstrating an insatiable appetite for all news related to these topics. Become the in-house expert on topics that are a part of your brand and important to your manager. Be the lightning rod of information. Anticipate things that could be relevant to your manager and send an executive summary of what you learn. Be the first to read and summarize any consultant report, white paper, or industry survey within your scope for your manager. Own your AOR— no excuses. This will further establish your credibility and expertise in your manager's eyes and enable you to provide valuable insights and innovative solutions.

- **Network and collaborate with colleagues.** Reach out and connect with colleagues who are also focused on goals that are aligned with your brand. By collaborating with others, you can expand your knowledge, learn from their experiences, and develop new opportunities to showcase your expertise.

- **Be proactive and take the lead.** Volunteer for projects or tasks that align with your personal brand and manager's goals. By consistently delivering high-quality work and demonstrating your passion and commitment, you will become the go-to person whenever your manager requires assistance or expertise in your specific areas.

- **Communicate your brand effectively.** Ensure that your manager and colleagues are aware of your expertise and how it aligns with their goals or the firm's objectives. This can be done through regular updates, sharing relevant articles or insights, or participating in meetings or forums where you can showcase your knowledge and provide valuable input, ensuring you reflect the pillars of the brand in everything you do (creating a ripple effect).

- **Seek advice and evaluate progress.** Regularly seek advice from your manager (N+1), manager's manager (N+2), peers, and other stakeholders to gauge how well your brand is perceived and if there are any areas for improvement. Take this advice constructively and make necessary adjustments to further strengthen your personal brand.

Many people make the mistake of never developing the mindset of "What can I do to help my boss succeed?" If you want to succeed, make yourself invaluable to your boss. Stay aligned with their goals and do not let your emotions overcome you when their goals and priorities change. That is life in a dynamic organization; you must go with the flow and roll with it when the situation changes (more on this to come in Chapter 13, where we honor Bruce Lee's concept to "be like water").

Avoid the defensive posture some take because they feel sorry for themselves after putting a lot of work into something that is no longer relevant. It may be tough on you, but guess what? It's probably even harder on your boss, so get over it. Don't be myopic about the time and effort you put into something that's no longer a top priority. Don't expend energy complaining, defending, or explaining how much time you have put into the project. It's a sunk cost. The commander's objective has changed. Get on with the execution of the new mission. Don't dwell in the past.

RULE 2: IT'S NOT ABOUT YOU

Know that it's not personal. Decision-making is imperfect. No firm or manager makes the perfect decision every time, and you must understand that are myriad inputs into each decision. In addition, the decision may not be at the sole discretion of your manager. Oftentimes, different stakeholders are involved in the decision process, from human capital partners to peer-level managers in other lines of business. Sometimes, outside governmental bodies, other geographies, and senior management may have their own preferred outcomes. Store this in the dedicated Elite Performance Pillars™ compartment of your brain and remember that when the next reorganization announcement is made, or the next promotion is granted, or the next change in role and responsibilities occurs, it's not about you.

As a recent example, one of my executive coaching clients was employed at a financial firm that acquired another firm. Once the acquisition closed, her firm integrated the personnel from the acquired firm into the organization. In that process, there was the inevitable reshuffle, which resulted in a manager from the acquired firm being put in charge of the business unit my client was in. For my client, it appeared personal. The outcome was that she had a new manager in a role that she envisioned for herself. However, the reality of the decision process was much more complex than that. With any acquisition, the aim is to create value for the shareholders by acquiring the target firm's human capital, intellectual property, market prowess, customer base, and other things.

In this case, executive C-suite level management wanted to ensure that the acquired management had fair representation across the business lines. HR played its role by making sure that the business implemented the directive of executive management to ensure key managers from the acquired firm were given management roles in the combined business units. In isolation, without any outside perspective, my client was at risk of taking the decision personally and seeing it as a lack of confidence in her abilities.

During my career, there were several times I was on the receiving end of a decision, just like my client. Even if you realize such a decision was not personal, it may still sting. However, always remember that you will never be privy to the multitude of inputs that go into the decisions that directly impact you. As I had told myself in the past, the decision was most likely not about me, and I reminded my client of the same advice.

Instead of fixating on the decision, we discussed the multiple factors at work, from the need to create value for the shareholders to executive management taking measures to ensure the talent acquired in the deal was not only retained but given management roles. We also considered that throughout the process, this was monitored by HR, who reviewed the relevant metrics. This is an illustration of how complex the inner workings of a corporate decision can be and why it is not about you. Play the long game and keep a seat at the table.

Oftentimes in our careers when we do not receive the promotion we were expecting and someone else above us is hired, our reaction can be to take this personally. We may feel we deserve it or are better qualified for the role, but remember, it is not about you. There are a variety of imperfect inputs in decisions with any firm. The reality is that you may never know or understand what the modus operandi or decision-making process was, the reason, or the causality of the outcome. The average person may, understandably, tend to personalize it. They see this as the organization making a direct vote against them or as a setback to their career progression.

Unequivocally, I can assure you from my multiple decades involved in management changes and different business integrations that, more often than not, this decision was not about you. But as an elite performer, you can challenge the assumption and take into consideration that if it was about you, then this is the time to gain perspective. What do you need to do now to change the perception people may have of you?

Now is the time to take a personal inventory and obtain advice from trusted colleagues or, if you're using an executive coaching firm, your coach to increase your personal awareness. Decide with your coach the one or two things you want to work on personally mastering. Every tool you sharpen goes into your personal mastery toolbox.

As an elite performer, if you make the conscious choice to form a positive mindset and understand that there is a remote chance this decision was about you, then this is the time to act and realize what course you will set for the journey ahead. By intentionally investing in one's personal tool kit and professional development, individuals can improve how they are perceived and increase their value to the organization. The next time you're in pursuit of the position that you aspire to be in, you will have invested in your personal tool kit and further enhanced the perception of who you are and your valuable contribution to the firm. As a reminder, when I work with my clients, I advise them to invest in the best return on investments—themselves. That consists of two aspects: (1) a personal tool kit and (2) professional development. By honing one's skills and advancing professionally, individuals can attain a level of elite performance and realize their aspirations.

Let's return to the earlier example of a manager from an acquired firm being put in a management position in the newly formed business unit. In situations like this, you as an elite performer must realize there is another scenario happening behind the scenes that I have witnessed frequently throughout my career. Sometimes, there is a compromise in the decision process. Perhaps there was extensive discussion about the new manager and the need to retain them in a management role. However, unbeknownst to you, during the discussions, your manager was a strong advocate for you; highlighted several of your accolades; and stated that you're very reliable, dedicated, and selfless.

In the short term, you could perceive the announced change as negative and see it as working against you because you are not receiving the promotion on the timeline that you aspired to. It is natural to feel this way, but I would like to reassure you that this change does not necessarily signify a roadblock to your professional goals. There may still be avenues for growth and progression.

Elite players know they benefit from staying calm during the announcements of reorganizations because they know what they don't know. What you may not know is that the discussion behind those closed doors could go something like this: "We really count on Danielle. I think she's ready, and she exhibits all the qualities we want at this firm that justify enlarging her mandate and empowering her to really broaden her managerial responsibilities. However, at this point, it's critical to make sure that we have a successful integration, and the manager that we acquired from the new firm needs to be seen as equal in the new management structure. Once this is completed, I think Danielle is our number one choice for taking on more responsibility in the new year. Let's rebalance the management structure now and focus on successful integration today. We can then set the trajectory of how we want Danielle to be further empowered in the new year."

Believe me, I have participated in many of those trade-offs where you aim to settle things down for now and make bold plans for the future. Now, if you're Danielle, and you don't have the context (which, most likely, you won't) so you personalize this decision and then start to act in an inappropriate way, it can be catastrophic. You have a tailwind of goodwill behind you. Not only do you have your manager but several other managers really advocating for continued progression in your career while collectively realizing the primary goal at present is the successful integration of the acquisition in all aspects.

There is strong agreement across the management team that they want to see you grow and take on more responsibility in the near future. But you forget that it's not about you, and instead, you start to act defiant, visibly disappointed, and make your frustrations known to your managers and others. Just as management is focused on making the integration a success, your antics undermine their efforts, and frustrations build. Questions start to arise that maybe you aren't the person they thought you were. Just as you had a strong tailwind of support heading into the new year, it quickly fades.

Elite performers do not score their own goals, so don't tarnish your brand. Remember that decisions and reorganizations are most likely not about you. However, rest assured that senior management, via the transformation of the business, wants to achieve the desired outcome. This is your opportunity to shine. Make a genuine effort to support the newly appointed management. Ask yourself, if you had been awarded this management role, what would you like to see from the person that would be in the role you are occupying today? Then, do it! Exceed expectations and be an enabler. Create the position that you want to be in. I advise all of my clients to maximize their optionality. Even if you want to consider outside roles, you will still want to follow the steps above to best position yourself for the future in your present position at the firm.

One month after the announcement, when senior management asks the manager, "How is it going?" you want the new manager to say, "I wasn't sure how it was going to work with (insert your name), but they have gone out of their way to be helpful in the transition." This positive feedback will get back to your manager, and in this critical integration period, you will distinguish yourself by supporting management's plan to make it work. The success of the acquisition is far more important than anyone's individual career. You know the changes were not about you, but if you align your efforts with senior management's priority to make it work by thinking ahead and playing it smart, this will also benefit your career. Management changes may impact you, but elite performers continue to chart that positive course ahead and focus on their personal mastery and professional development.

By not taking the decisions personally, elite performers continue to strive. They align themselves with senior management's big-picture goals and move forward in their careers. Stay focused throughout the process and realize that decisions are always imperfect. Be the person that senior management points to as to why their decision was a success. Thus, by helping your manager, you are helping your own career.

RULE 3: PLAY ON YOUR TOES

Anticipate needs and take initiative. However busy you may think you are, realize that your manager is busier. In recognizing this, your goal is to make things easier for your boss. I have witnessed many times, either in the workplace or as a coach, people getting frustrated because their manager was not fully aware of what they were doing.

First, because your manager is busy, it's hard to follow what other people are doing, so keep your boss informed. Give yourself your own litmus test. How aware are you of your direct reports' activities, accomplishments, challenges, and issues they are facing?

My point is that the onus is on you. Communicate openly and succinctly with your boss. Every Sunday was my mark to market, when I documented where I stood with respect to my three to five priorities from my perspective. Using a Hoshin Kanri grading system, I would denote the status as red, yellow, or green.[25]

Most importantly, I made it a point to provide my manager with up-to-date status reports regarding my objectives and what I was working on every Sunday evening. This acted as a weekly update of where I was on my key aims and identified areas where I may need his help or have an issue of concern. By using bullet points and ensuring that the update was no more than one page, I made the report succinct, thereby making it easy to understand and digest. Overall, it helped me to stay focused on my goals and ensure that I was making progress toward achieving them.

This also helped my manager to anticipate the unknown unknowns (made famous by former Secretary of Defense Donald Rumsfeld) and provided him with the most

25   The Art of Service. *Hoshin Kanri A Complete Guide.* Hoshin Kanri Publishing, 2020.

up-to-date status of key items that were within my area of responsibility. You have no idea how your boss's world has changed since you last saw them, but at least by taking this initiative, there is one less surprise for them. Making the effort to provide them with a succinct snapshot of your activities also stimulates their own thought process regarding how some recent changes may impact your priorities. Again, it is about making the effort to make work efficient for your manager.

As part of your commitment to spend 5–10 percent of your time on planning your career as an elite performer, take time to look out over the horizon. Starting with your brand and your three to five FAST objectives, what things do you anticipate will undergo significant change in the near future, and what steps do you believe are necessary to prepare for and adapt to these changes starting today? Identify those items, trends, and concerns and how they will impact the business as opportunities or threats. Challenge yourself to look beyond the tactical events of this quarter and think more strategically about how the business may change and what you need to do today to start to prepare. This may involve investing in new technologies, adopting more sustainable practices, or exploring new markets and customer segments. By taking proactive steps today, you can help ensure the firm is well-positioned to thrive in the years to come.

Share these thoughts with your boss as a good steward of the firm, and express your willingness to get involved under their guidance. This is another benefit of committing time to think about and plan your career. Without this commitment, it is easy to fall into the rut of just being task-oriented without ever thinking strategically and getting labeled as such. Anticipating your manager's needs by developing a briefing document for an upcoming client meeting or helping them prepare for their meeting with their boss is what I call playing on the balls of your feet. You are agile and ready to pivot depending on the needs of the business and your manager.

In addition, you need to demonstrate grit, because sometimes, it takes sheer determination and drive to get things done. Embrace Robin Sharma's motto: "World-class begins where your comfort zone ends."[26] Put yourself out there and be willing to do what others avoid. Or to state it differently, take on the most difficult and demanding jobs, projects, or clients when there is an actual opportunity, and demonstrate the sheer tenacity to see it through. Fundamentally, it is about adopting a mindset to serve. If they are genuine and true, your actions will shine like a beacon of light.

RULE 4: BLOCK EVERY SHOT

Never let your manager be blindsided. Think back to my first manager's quote: "This job is as simple or as difficult as you want to make it." If you're a soccer/football fan, picture yourself as the sweeper. You're the last defender before the goalie and your aim is to protect the goal. Keep your eyes and ears open at all times. What things are you learning from clients, peers, and other divisions within the firm that could impact your manager's business? Get in front of these topics, be they positive opportunities for growth and expansion or potentially negative issues that will require lead time to rectify.

Managers quickly get to know which people are looking out for them and doing their best to prevent them from getting blindsided. Every day, you suit up and play on the corporate field. Be the left guard in American football every day you suit up. The left guard is one of the five members of

---

26 Sharma, Robin. *The 5AM Club: Own Your Morning. Elevate Your Life.* Harpercollins Publishers, 2018.

the offensive line and plays just to the left of the center. The left guard has dual responsibility: (1) blocking defenders on almost every play; and (2) protecting the quarterback from the nearest defenders, trying to provide the quarterback just a fraction of a second more time so they can read the field and make the best play given the situation. It's typically one of the highest-paid offensive line positions. Starting quarterbacks in the NFL are predominantly right-handed, so the left side is their blindside on the football field. Be the left guard for your boss. Protect his blindside. Buy them some time so they can execute the best plan.

RULE 5: OWN IT—DON'T EXPECT HANDHOLDING FROM YOUR BOSS

In the US military, helicopters are configured for a crew of two: a pilot and a combination copilot-gunner. To ensure there is clear communication in the cockpit when flight controls are transferred within the aircraft, the pilot flying will ask the other pilot, "You have the controls?" The receiving pilot will place their hand on the controls and affirm the question by stating, "I have the controls." This ensures there is no miscommunication and that someone is flying the aircraft at all times. The pilot flying does not release the controls until the receiving pilot verifies that they have the controls.

The stakes are high in a military aircraft. Take the same approach in the work environment. When your manager gives you the controls, own it like a pilot in command. Take the controls and fly the mission, but be sure to clarify the commander's intent and validate their desired end state. We discussed the commander's intent earlier in Pillar II: Being a Better Manager. As a reminder, in the military, the commander's intent is the commander's personal expression of the purpose of the operation, a broad description and definition of a successful mission. It consists of three elements: (1) why—the purpose, (2) how—the method, and (3) the goal—the end state of the battlefield.

When you take the controls, be sure to confirm that you have a clear and current understanding of your manager's why, how, and goal for the mission. To minimize the risk of drifting off course, keep your manager informed of your progress. If you do get stuck, reach out promptly for their guidance to get back on course. Most importantly, engage and generate some forward momentum so your manager knows you have the controls and are focused on the mission. As General MacArthur instructed the West Point cadets, "[Have] an appetite for adventure over love of ease."[27]

RULE 6: BE AMAZINGLY PREDICTABLE

Deliver on time, every time. If you're committed to developing your personal brand, then being amazingly predictable is the best advertising campaign you can ever have. Your manager faces countless issues and uncertainties every day. Be the one constant they can depend on. This is a core principle of an AOR. Do so and deliver to the highest standard.

When I was in finance, managing some 600 salespeople globally, I was often dismayed by people who consistently failed to meet the deadlines for mandatory compliance courses. These were online courses that we were usually given months to accomplish. Financial regulators held the bank accountable for maintaining high standards with regard to anti-money laundering and other regulated matters. Both my manager and I were some of the most frequent travelers in the bank, which meant we had less time to do the

27 Kenneth Abramowitz, "General MacArthur's Speech to Cadets at the U.S. Military Academy, 1962," Save the West, May 25, 2020, https://savethewest.com/douglas-macarthurs-speech-to-cadets-at-the-u-s-military-academy-1962/.

online courses. But neither of us made excuses. Sometimes, it meant staying late on a Friday night or coming in on the weekend to complete the courses, but we did it and completed the required training on time, every time. Compliance monitored the completion rate and notified the manager if one of their employees was at risk of missing the deadline. Managers would then chase the employee to remind them that a specific course was still not completed. Some would miss the deadline and we would have to send more chasers ex post facto. Often, the people who were most concerned about their bonus were the same people who would be penalized 5–10 percent of their bonus for failing to complete a straightforward and mandatory compliance exam. Who are you going to trust, to extend greater responsibility to, to promote?

You can think about it like Pavlov's dogs, but understand that Pavlovian responses are not limited to dogs exclusively. Many of you may recall that in Pavlov's experiments, he trained dogs to salivate when they heard a bell by pairing the bell sound with food. The bell became a stimulus that triggered a conditioned response of salivation, even without food present. In simple terms, two stimuli can be linked together to produce a new learned response in a person or animal. Pavlov's classical conditioning can also apply to human psychology, or more specifically, to your manager.

If employee A consistently fails to meet deadlines, doesn't do what they say they will do, or fails to own a task assigned to them, this becomes classical conditioning (a.k.a. Pavlovian) for your manager. The manager learns that employee A will most likely fail to meet deadlines, need reminding, and may not take ownership of key tasks. This conditioned response by your manager may be fair or unfair, but you can control it by owning what you are asked to do, meeting or beating every deadline you are given, and simply demonstrating aptitude through your actions. Instead of saying what you are going to do, just do it! Essentially, don't be employee A. Own what you're asked to do.

RULE 7: NO MANAGER WANTS MORE PROBLEMS, SO DON'T BE A PROBLEM

Managers have enough problems of their own. Do not add to their list by being another problem. What do I mean? Do not be the person who walks into their boss's office and habitually points out all the things that are going wrong. This is self-sabotage. You might as well just fall on a career grenade and explode. Instead, be the person who makes observations and comes up with suggestions. Have a discussion with your boss and always follow the restaurant approach by offering a menu of potential solutions. This approach creates a win-win situation. More often than not, the manager is aware of the problem but has not had a chance to implement a solution.

In comparison, a complaining employee adds little value by simply identifying issues and will suffer from a double negative effect:

- Negative effect number one: The Pavlovian conditional response will strike again. Their manager will see the employee come down the hallway and will anticipate the conditional response before the employee even enters their office. This person is negative energy incarnate. I'm not saying you must be a cheerleader, but don't consistently be the problem person.

- Negative effect number two: Over time, the manager will form a mental callus with regard to discussions with the employee and simply tune out their input.

A different way to think about rule seven is to see the other as they see themself. Raise your self-awareness and put yourself in your manager's shoes. Ask yourself how you would like to be on the receiving end of habitual complaints.

One of the truisms that I discovered as I advanced in my career was that you are better off staying calm and not causing drama during stressful times. Earlier in my career, I would see things, evaluate the proposed reorganization, and tell myself that I was putting the firm first or that I cared enough to speak out and identify the potential risks embedded in the decision for the good of the firm. In theory, expressing your concerns for the firm is a good idea, and I believed in the sentiment. But over time, I came to realize I had access to a limited information set and viewed the decision through my personal lens. So, I made an assumption: for the most part, the people I worked for were quite intelligent and motivated. Let's take that as a basic truth. Now, pay attention to my words carefully. I'm not saying I liked everyone or trusted everyone, but I had to admit to myself that most of the people I worked for were intelligent.

Here is the punch line: the next time frustration peaks and you don't understand the logic of the decision, remember your base assumption that your management is intelligent, so perhaps something else is going on. Resist the temptation to prepare your mental legal case and argue fact by fact in your head about why you are right. Becoming preoccupied with something, overthinking it, and overanalyzing it is not good for your job, your relationship with your manager, or your personal health. The realization should be that you don't see it, or more specifically, you don't see it through their vantage point.

Instead, you see it through your lens. The fact is that your perspective is different. The first thing you must realize is that you'll never completely know what the modus operandi is vis-à-vis the people above you or the firm, more generally speaking. When something doesn't make sense, there are usually just different priorities. It's possible that something above you is happening that you don't have access to yet, which could explain the confusion. It's important to keep an open mind and try to gather as much information as possible before making any assumptions or judgments. Likewise, senior management doesn't have a crystal ball, nor do they necessarily have access to perfectly comprehensive information.

When people fail to step back to take that perspective and resist letting go of trying to figure things out, it's their downfall. The tipping point for me came when I found myself in these situations. I would exercise the following thought process: The firm I work for and the people I work for are quite intelligent. Ergo, this decision, which doesn't make sense to me, must make sense to someone. I may not understand the modus operandi behind that today, but I'm not going to expend further energy fighting it, challenging it, or rationalizing it. The other benefit of accepting this outcome is that it allowed me to more quickly transition to other priorities and not get stuck in a rut that I could not control.

Take solace in the fact that your management is intelligent. Do not waste energy challenging them at every junction. Leave room to contribute to strategic innovation, but accept that there are many unknown unknowns. Then, work with it.

This idea is a little bit of yin-yang from my martial arts days. Martial artists use the yin-yang theory to harmonize their movements, balance their strengths and weaknesses, and adapt to different situations. You can't always be on the attack. Sometimes you need to step back and then strike. Elite performers emulate this same energy flow in the work world.

Not every decision, hire, organizational change, and so forth, is going to make sense to you, and you can expend a lot of energy if you wrestle with each one of these. I would suggest that you take a step back and conserve your energy. Be calm in times of chaos, and accept these outcomes. Every once in a while, when the situation merits, you can engage and respectfully challenge. Limit your engagement to topics that are closely related to your personal brand so that it is consistent with core competencies and areas of expertise.

When I was the global head of sales and the firm made a policy change that impacted clients, I would selectively engage in a constructive manner. In these situations, I would say something like, "If we would like to obtain some initial feedback on our potential decision before implementation, I would be happy to arrange these meetings with key clients."

Scarcity has value, and by being very selective in your engagements, you will shift the balance, as you will rarely challenge the status quo. People will naturally be drawn in because they know you are selective and must have something significant to contribute.

In working with your manager, remember that there is a built-in gyroscope within each of us, our internal GPS. The moment we stop complaining, stop fighting the change, our mind is freed up. It's like deleting the cache on a computer. You will think more clearly and sharply, and you will move forward. This is innate to us. So, be the solution, accept change, and don't be the problem.

RULE 8: MIRROR COMMUNICATION

Communicate the way your manager prefers to communicate. While working at a European bank for more than two decades, the concept of mirroring was complicated. Not only did I face a cultural and educational difference but also a language difference. In addition to these factors, each firm has its own culture, just as every manager has their own style. I knew it was imperative to understand each of these aspects of the managers in my chain of command if I was going to perform at an elite level.

Mirroring communication involves imitating both the verbal and nonverbal cues of another person to show identification and understanding. Go one step further to improve the effectiveness of your communication and pay particular attention to repetitive phrases, mantras, and specific words.

At each presentation given by a senior manager, I would take notes on my phone of not only the words and phrases they selected but also the cadence they used and how they presented. In particular, one of the senior managers was very methodical. To me, it was reminiscent of a physics problem at university where you had to show all of your work. If you missed a step, points were deducted. My presentations changed. I spoke to ensure information was presented sequentially and I justified every step in the process.

However, mirroring does not always work, and one has to be careful about how literal descriptions can appear out of context. The financial world in and of itself is another language with its own dictionary of acronyms.

With advancements in trading systems and digitization, the bank reorganized the credit area of our fixed-income business. The liquidity (the ease with which we could trade, buy, or sell a product) of credit instruments continued to improve, as did the frequency with which clients were trading these products. During the reorganization, the hours were long. People worked hard and tried to make the resultant restructuring easily understood. We reviewed the new names of the different groups with the aim of being as self-explanatory as possible. The result was that the new sales and trading client group was assigned a name that literally described the activity: "the frequent user client desk." It may have been an accurate description that mirrored the activity, but I expressed some concerns over the acronym. We made a modification and decided to drop "user" in the new name for the activity.

In today's digital world, you have to pay particular attention to capturing your manager's attention at the beginning of the discussion and know their preferences and tendencies when you present. Some managers want you to take them through the details, while others have short attention spans that require you to draw them in early. In either situation, you must know your audience and use mirroring techniques to be an effective communicator with your manager.

Let's go behind the scenes to look at the science behind mirroring communication. It is based on the concept of mirror neurons, which are brain cells that fire when we observe or perform an action. Mirror neurons help us to learn from others, empathize with them, and predict their intentions. When we mirror someone's body language, tone, or words, we activate the same mirror neurons in their brain, creating a sense of similarity and alignment. Mirroring has long been used in sales, as it can help to build rapport, trust, and connection with the other person by making them feel heard and validated.

Research in psychology has linked posture mirroring, a key element of nonverbal behavior, to rapport and empathy, supporting effective communication. In addition, Dr. Nemko, published in *Psychology Today*, found that mirroring your conversation partner's speech patterns can also be a helpful way to facilitate more effective communication."[28]

Emails require the same discipline. Each manager has a style. Find out or ask your manager what works best for them and follow their guidance. I will make one important point on this topic that may save your job someday: write every email as if it can be forwarded to anyone.

Trust me, emails can go to anyone within the firm, so be thoughtful and choose your words carefully because they can find their way to the inbox of unintended readers. Last, you should know that many companies today run software that looks for keywords in all electronic communications, so be smart and remember that digital communication is permanent.

RULE 9: GIVE 'EM A BREAK

Try giving your boss the benefit of the doubt. One of the most important rules is that, like you, managers are only human. Guess what? That means they're not perfect! Neither are you, so give your manager a break once in a while.

There are a few people who will ask their boss late on a Friday at the end of a long week, "Is there anything I can do to help you over the weekend?" The statement speaks for itself. Only top performers reach out with sincerity, recognizing their boss also had a long week, and genuinely offer to help.

There will be other moments when your boss reaches out to you as you're walking out the door to do something urgent for them before you head home that evening. You can be upset and frustrated that they just told you or give

---

28 Marty Nemko Ph.D., "The Power of Mirroring," *Psychology Today*, October 31, 2021, https://www.psychologytoday.com/us/blog/how-do-life/202110/the-power-mirroring.

them the benefit of the doubt. Your boss just finished a three-hour board meeting during which an urgent situation arose, and they could only get to it now, but it needs immediate attention.

I have worked with some excellent managers, but I have never met a manager who could read my mind. Breaking news: your manager can't read your mind, either! Give your manager a break, and at the right time, share your longer-term ambitions, your flexibility regarding geographic locations, and any special family situations with them. This is important because it allows them to better understand your situation so that when opportunities arise, it eliminates the guessing game, and they can be proactive in exploring a potential fit for both you and the firm.

Give your boss a break if you never shared with them that your dream job is to work in Asia and they transferred one of your colleagues. Helping your boss when they need a lifeline regarding the workload, lifting their spirits when things do not go the right way, and sharing your professional ambitions with them will all go a long way in respecting your manager as a person.

RULE 10: PUSH AND PULL

Push to get pulled. A critical part of your relationship with your manager is your mindset. Perhaps there are few ideal managers, but our base assumption is that your manager is trying to do their job. They are trying to perform. They're trying to create value for the firm. This is one key tenet of success you must truly be aligned with in order to help your boss succeed.

Be careful with the expenditure of your own political capital. I am not suggesting that you compromise who you are, but many times, you don't know the meeting your boss just had, what happened during their day, or the other issues they're dealing with.

Let's get back to maintaining intellectual integrity. You can assume one thing with a high level of confidence: your manager has greater responsibilities than you do. Respect that. One key tenet is to ask yourself, "How can I help make my boss successful?" Be honest and open about what things you can do that will help them succeed in meeting the demands that the organization puts on them. This is a great way to become invaluable. As you push to help them succeed, they form a positive bias toward you. By doing so, you set yourself up for success. The mental imagery you should form is that you are pushing someone's car that is stuck in the snow, helping them to gain traction and drive away.

The core concept of push and pull is to ensure that you're delivering and *pushing* things that are aligned with what your boss needs. This will create a cause-and-effect dynamic: the better you get at producing products desired by your boss and pushing them down the conveyor belt, the more they will *pull* from you, creating a positive reliance on your ability to push forward to get things done.

CHAPTER 11 **TAKEAWAYS**

- The Top Ten Rules of Managing Your Manager for Elite Performers:

  1. Know what's important.
  2. It's not about you: know it's not personal.
  3. Play on your toes: anticipate needs and take initiative.
  4. Block every shot: never let your manager be blindsided.
  5. Own it: don't expect handholding from your boss.
  6. Be amazingly predictable: deliver on time, every time.
  7. No manager wants more problems, so don't be a problem.
  8. Mirror communication: communicate the way they prefer to communicate.
  9. Give 'em a break: try giving your boss the benefit of the doubt.
  10. Push and pull: push to get pulled.

THE ART OF BEING MALLEABLE—PUSH AND PULL

"What is more malleable is always superior over that which is immovable. This is the principle of controlling things by going along with them, of mastery through adaptation."
—LAO TZU

LAO TZU'S QUOTE expresses the idea that being malleable can give one an advantage over those who are fixed and unyielding because it allows one to adjust to the changing situations and influence them in one's favor. This is a continuation of rule ten: push and pull.

Be malleable to your manager's needs. Deadlines change, projects get canceled, and urgent situations occur. Your willingness to adapt and bend your schedule to your manager's needs will strengthen your relationship and make you an asset. You want to be on the shortlist so that when your manager is in a pinch and needs someone they trust to step up and own the topic; you, as an elite performer, will be at the top of the list.

Don't make the mistake I've seen of trying to be the invisible man. You never fool anyone, at least over a sustained period, as there are always individuals who conveniently avoid the epicenter of the action. They're traveling and aren't contactable, or they wait to check their email or delay their response. I know one thing in life holds true: the truth always comes out.

Flexibility is critical in today's dynamic business world, so push and pull in everything you do. Push yourself to be excellent in everything that has your brand on it, and be willing to be pulled when your manager needs you. Push forward through the difficult times and build momentum so you can sustain it over the next hill. Think about what you can do better to help your boss succeed. Sometimes that means getting up on your toes and, through sheer grit and determination, helping push the cart up the hill. In each of these actions, a correlation is formed. For your manager, there's a positive correlation: when there's a challenge and the team faces an uphill battle, they know you're there to help push through and get over the apex of the hill.

Now, get ready for the pull. The next time your boss gets promoted or is asked to take on an additional duty, they will pull you along to help advance their career as well as your own. Through push and pull, you can form this symbiotic relationship whereby their success can enable your success. As your manager rises, they create a pulling force. Like drafting in Formula 1 racing, you reduce the drag or friction you are subjected to in your career by being pulled in your manager's slipstream, thus reducing the overall resistance in your journey to your next milestone.

A note for emerging stars and young professionals: push and pull will also work for you if you heed this additional advice. At the earlier stages in your career, it's critical to understand exactly what your boss is asking of you and to then make sure you don't go too far down a path (with good intent) without checking in. Regarding checking in, there are different temperaments that you will be exposed to, so do it in a mindful way. Make sure that you provide succinct updates, but not too frequently, allowing your manager to easily understand where you are going and the approach you are taking.

Ensure you use your network. Have a fresh pair of eyes review your work. Ask them if your content is clear and whether they understand the approach you are taking for the project.

If you are under pressure and simply do not have time to receive feedback from a third party, take a fifteen-minute break to review the document or presentation from front to back and read it out loud. Always double-check the math and perform a sanity check before sending it to your boss.

At all costs, you want to avoid heading blindly down a road without keeping your boss updated as the deadline approaches, especially when your project is far away from the desired end state. Periodic progress updates will save you—and, ultimately, your manager—a lot of frustration by avoiding the situation where they face a deadline and your work misses the target.

HOW TO GET A PROMOTION

This is push and pull in action again. In my executive coaching business, I have worked with several clients on the specific planning steps elite performers take that many overlook in their zeal to get promoted and then wonder why they did not receive the promotion ex post facto. I have also worked with clients who did not work with me prior to the recent promotion decision, and we walked it back to see how they could improve for next time.

Oftentimes, when I speak with clients who did not get promoted, they voice their frustration to me that even though they are one of the hardest working members of the team and their business unit consistently exceeds expectations, they did not receive the promotion. The first thing I tell them is that if what they're telling me is true, then their promotion is a problem for their manager. The unsaid truth is that when a performing and dependable staff member gets promoted, the void that they create upon being promoted is an issue. Many people do not consider how their promotion will impact their boss. They stymie their career because their (conscious or unconscious) approach is "me, me, me," missing the salient point that their desire to advance has repercussions for their manager.

Critical thinking is required for at least twelve months to create a forward path that provides a solution to fill your void and give your manager confidence that the results will still be delivered as you transition to a new role. You must develop a succession plan that takes into account numerous inputs, such as the successor's fit for the role, their fit and familiarity with your current manager, and awareness of the diversity and inclusion needs of the firm. Help your boss by having a plan to replace you so that your promotion is not a problem for them. Having a succession plan is different than having a *viable* succession plan. The time to start is now. Identify a successor that you think can meet your criteria and the needs of your manager. In your next one-on-one, ask the individual about their aspirations and whether they could see themselves in your role. Be honest about the demands of your job, travel requirements, and the expectations your boss has for the role. Answer any of their questions, and then ask them if they would like to be considered as your potential successor. Do not assume this is what they want. They need to affirm their desire and convince you that they have the potential to grow into your role.

During one of your formal meetings with your boss, be it a mid-year or end-of-year review or the equivalent, update them on your succession plan. It is important to receive their initial feedback, depending on their knowledge of the individual. If they're not familiar with that individual, offer to arrange a coffee chat or informal meeting for the two of them. Let your manager know that you will be investing your time in developing this rising star because you believe there is potential for this person to replace you at the right time in the future. This is the push part of a promotion that many people skip. They do not push for solutions that will make the transition smooth and effective for their manager.

Instead, it's all about "promote me," "here's why I should be promoted," and so forth. Put a little effort into creating a pulling force from your manager. If someone has not demonstrated the maturity or the professional integrity to develop a well-thought-out succession plan, why would they want to promote them?

Internal promotions are tricky. Every firm purports to espouse the mantra that they want to promote from within. It may be true, but the onus is on you, as a good steward of the firm, to anticipate the transition and provide a win-win solution. What they *don't* tell you about getting a promotion is to look at it from your manager's point of view. If you are not planning at least twelve months ahead, you are not equipping your boss to help pull you into the next role. Own and push forward a well-thought-out succession plan to enable your manager to pull you into your next promotion when the opportunity arises.

The following scene is repeated across business settings around the world: During an offsite meeting as a senior manager, I was discussing my plans with a colleague from Asia. He mentioned his need for a high-performing manager who matched a profile on my team. My response was that John Doe on my team would be an ideal fit for the role. However, with no succession plan in place, I couldn't afford to lose him. It's that quickly that a career opportunity can be missed. My colleague from Asia respected me and didn't want to take advantage and leave me worse off, so he called his favorite headhunter to discuss a search.

Elite performers don't make a succession plan simply a paper exercise. As an elite performer, you begin mentoring your protégé and providing periodic progress reports to your boss. At the mid-year review, you update your manager that Sue is making excellent progress, demonstrating strong leadership skills on the projects she is driving, and that you recently received positive feedback from team members who attended the on-site meeting she hosted. You tell your boss that you would appreciate their opinion regarding her preparedness for the role and ask to find a convenient time for the two of them to have a business dinner together. The dinner goes well, and you mutually discuss a few items that Sue can work on in the second half of the year. For example, your boss would like her to present to his executive committee meeting in September.

You continue pushing to develop Sue and help her prepare to succeed in the new role. During your year-end review, you inform your boss that you believe she could fill your shoes when the time is right. Your boss says, "That's great news. We need new senior leadership in Asia as the current head is planning to take a new role in the firm next year." He further shares that they would prefer to promote from within, and he would be pleased to endorse you for the Asia role now that—thanks to you—Sue is ready to step in and do an excellent job.

This is a powerful application of the push-and-pull career-management technique that elite performers use. Things do not happen by chance. In the situation above, you make yourself a more valuable asset not just to your manager but to the firm overall. By deciding to take action and push your business forward by developing your protégé, you've increased the agility of the firm and created positive career optionality for yourself. Being malleable and adapting your approach to the promotion process enables you to gain control of your career through adaptation.

CHAPTER 12 **TAKEAWAYS**

- Be malleable to your manager's needs. Your willingness to adapt and bend to your manager's needs will strengthen your relationship and make you an asset.

- Flexibility is critical in today's dynamic business world, so push and pull in everything you do. Push yourself to be excellent in everything that has your brand on it and be willing to be pulled when your manager needs you.

- Through push and pull, you can form a symbiotic relationship in which your manager's success enables your success. Like drafting in Formula 1 racing, as your manager rises, they create a pulling force in their slipstream.

PART V

CONCLUSION

BACK TO YOU: BEGIN WITH THE END IN MIND

"We may be very busy, we may be very efficient, but we will also be truly effective only when we begin with the end in mind."
—STEPHEN R. COVEY

REVISITING YOU ON THE PATH TO GREATNESS

With your personal foundation built and mastery of the Elite Performance Pillars™ in progress, now is the time to examine your internal GPS.

What you internalize will determine your external trajectory. Your engine is your inner self; it's what drives you. It will manifest itself as your mantra, your brand. It's the essence of beginning with the end in mind.

Mental imagery is a powerful technique. Athletes at the elite level tap into the power of using mental imagery, like elite free solo climber Alex Honnold. He made the first free solo climb of El Capitan in Yosemite National Park in June 2017. Honnold trained by visualizing each grab of the ascent. His internal GPS set the goal of climbing the nearly three-thousand-foot granite wall of El Capitan, without any ropes or safety gear, in less than four hours, which many consider to be the greatest rock climbing feat in history.[29]

Just as it did for Honnold, mental imagery helps you improve your focus, anxiety management, skill mastery, and confidence. It involves using all the senses, not just

---

29 Mark Synnott, "Exclusive: Alex Honnold Completes the Most Dangerous Free-Solo Event Ever," *National Geographic,* October 3, 2018, https://www.nationalgeographic.com/adventure/article/most-dangerous-free-solo-climb-yosemite-national-park-el-capitan.

vision, to create a vivid and realistic mental image of the desired end state. I use mental imagery routinely in my day-to-day life, from visualizing my executive and strategy consulting business ExecPathfinders LLC's global reach in 2030 to how I will feel after the daily execution of my elite performance morning routine or, most recently, the image of myself surfing the waves of San Onofre, California.

It is imperative that you see yourself realizing your end goal, and mental imagery is a key motivator. If you are committed to being an elite performer, you need to be driven by a goal. What is the visualization of your goal? What do you want to achieve? Are your three to five professional goals clear? Make it so that these underpin the journey your internal GPS is taking you on, guiding and navigating you to your target. The Elite Performance Pillars™ require you to use the power of your mind to follow the step-by-step program and be supported by your convictions, drive, discipline, and self-accountability to achieve all of the success and happiness you deserve.

THE DESTINY OF MY INTERNAL GPS

We have spent time together reviewing the methodology of the Elite Performance Pillars™ step by step. Now that we know how to apply the EPP™ to achieve all the success and joy we deserve, let's find out our next destination in our journey.

Where is your internal GPS taking you? As we discussed earlier, your life and your career are a series of destinations. For me, it started under a desk flying imaginary planes and progressed to flying in the military. Then, my internal GPS set its sights on new destinations: a Cambridge MBA, pre-European Union, and then a career in international finance.

Be true to yourself throughout the journey, meaning that you should accept your weaknesses and own your strengths. Take comfort in this. There is only one amazing you on the planet, and that is how the Creator planned it.

Managing your career as an elite performer requires you to be brutally honest with yourself using the Right-Angle Rule (there is the person in the mirror, and God above is the referee to keep you honest, as He knows the truth). Be true to yourself when visualizing the characteristics of the destination for your career and your life. Play to your strengths, and find the unique blend of doing what you enjoy passionately that also happens to be your job. Yes, it's your dream job, but hopefully it came about through the process of silencing noise, advice, and biases from the past; being honest with yourself; and enthusiastically taking note of the characteristics that you want your job and your life to be composed of.

Today—right now—presents a unique opportunity to really explore your infinite potential. You have the chance to achieve your true joy and ultimate happiness by aligning your passions, skills, and motivations and then making the conscious commitment to seek out the best role such that you can enthusiastically put all of you to work every day, tapping into the things that you excel at and that come naturally to you.

To let your internal GPS truly choose the destination, you need to understand how your mind works. What is going on behind the curtain?

Not to be prescriptive, but use your senses to describe how you feel about the challenge of coding in a new language, creating that aerodynamic wing, or the thrill of interacting with people to conduct commerce. Focus on the description of the activities, not what is prescribed.

You must listen to your internal GPS in your comfortable chair, or on the sofa, or wherever you escape to, listening to music, or dreaming. Rely on instinct versus an analytical list of pros and cons. Trust your insights vs. data. Let go of the controls. The internal gyroscope will self-level the plane, and your internal GPS will guide you toward your next destination. Stay on your flight path until flying this leg of your career is fun and is on autopilot. Then it is on to the next destination on the journey of your life.

Succeeding at the Elite Performance Pillars™ requires self-accountability, which is complemented by the discipline to make incremental improvements each day that will enable you to transform your life in ways that you could not have previously envisioned. How do I know this? Because you have visualized the end state, told your inner self that these are your goals, and harnessed the power of your mind. Then, you've coupled these techniques with willpower, grit, and the daily commitment to move forward, step by step.

You will achieve the things that you now visualize because, each day, your built-in GPS will help you navigate toward the goal, the target that you have now clearly defined. The EPP™ is something I have been working on for over forty years, and I have now codified them so you can use them to achieve your life ambitions and joy.

Just like a pilot checking in periodically, the journey ahead will require you to continually hone in on your goal to confirm you are on course and making incremental corrections along the way. Remember that an aircraft's flight path is never a perfectly straight line, but if you as the pilot in command of your life continue to validate your goals and progress and take corrective actions to adjust your course en route, you will most certainly reach your destiny. The journey is about momentum. Yes, there will be setbacks, but for each step forward (and some backward), you make progress. Each of these experiences will go into your personal mastery tool kit.

My father instilled in me a simple reality—that he will not always be there for me—so I needed to set goals for myself, stay focused, and be committed so that if I fell down, I would have the resolve and determination to get back up.

However, I am not unique. We all face the same challenges. We all come from different circumstances, some more trying than others. Some may come from a protected bubble, but in due course, the bubble will be pricked. Those who come from trying circumstances may stay committed to their goal. Maybe their sweat equity will surpass many of our own doings, but the principle remains: begin with the end in mind. It's your life. Take ownership of it and you'll be truly amazed by what you can achieve.

There's much talk today about grit. It's something I greatly value and believe has immense merit. It's embedded in my process. Grit is like rough sandpaper going over a wood surface. At first, you start out with a coarse number to get rid of the large imperfections, and then, with continual repetition, you take out the imperfections, move up to a higher grade of sandpaper, and start to truly craft the piece of wood into a masterpiece.

Perhaps, at this stage of your career, many of you will find that you operate at a near-finished level of product quality. Now it's a finesse game in which you no longer use coarse sandpaper but the finest grade to shape your work. This finessing is the difference between something good and a true masterpiece. But don't be under any illusions; the EPP™ journey will not always be easy, nor will it always progress at your desired pace. Be resolute. This is where grit and the daily commitment to invest in yourself and your personal tool kit come into play. Know that, over time, you will improve, the elite performance morning routine will become a habit, and the habits will become part of the new you—the one you've visualized.

FOUR STEPS TO HELP YOU ON YOUR ELITE PERFORMANCE PILLARS™ JOURNEY

Step 1: PMA. Always maintain a Positive Mental Attitude. As Henry Ford famously said, "Whether you believe you can do a thing or not, you are right."[30]

No one starts at the finish line, so when you begin with the end in mind, know that no matter what journey you are on, from a one-hundred-meter race to an ultramarathon, achieving your goal will require you to cross the finish line. Each challenge will be different, and you will have to overcome certain obstacles, but all of that is just part of the journey.

I have completed fourteen marathons around the world, and one of my favorite things that really made marathons unique was my vantage point. It's quite a feeling to find yourself in the middle of Manhattan on Fifth Avenue heading south (safely), looking left and right in amazement, unencumbered by an onslaught of cars and tourists around you, just soaking up where you are. Take a look along your journey sometimes, and amaze yourself with where you are, the progress you have made, and simply the journey you are on.

Let this be your motivation. Each mile is part of the journey. Those of you who have done the New York City Marathon, that trek down Fifth Avenue to Central Park, know that the final miles remind you that New York City is not as flat as it looks on the map. There are other miles

---

30 Quoteresearch, "Whether You Believe You Can Do a Thing or Not, You Are Right," Quote Investigator, February 3, 2015, https://quoteinvestigator.com/2015/02/03/you-can/.

where you stride out, breathing easy and almost effortlessly floating, but your race will have these miles also.

Step 2: Whiteboard Goals. Marathon runners need to know where the finish line is. But long before that day, continual training is required. The first step is declaring you are going to run a marathon. Implicitly, this means you will need to train and determine your goal finish (sub-four hours, 3:30, etc.).

Whatever your goal is, you must declare it and write it down on your daily accountability plan (on a whiteboard, digital whiteboard, spreadsheet, etc.). This process is then repeated. My suggestion is to choose three to five FAST goals (as a reminder, FAST stands for frequently reviewed, ambitious, specific, and transparent) per major heading (again, my own categories are career, family, spiritual, and physical).

Taking the time to truly invest in yourself is a critical step. Many managers may find it unacceptable if their N-1s or the organization itself does not have clear goals, yet they have not defined their own professional, personal mastery, or physical goals. Some may, but 95 percent of the clients I work with admit that they don't take the necessary time to really reflect on their progress. It is important to find a quiet spot free of distractions like news, TV, computers, social media, and mobile phones. This allows you to make your own mark to market by taking stock of where you are on your journey, holding yourself accountable, and considering how others perceive your progress. It's an essential step in becoming an elite performer.

Ideally, you should reflect on your goals and ensure your internal GPS is tuned in precisely to your goals during your EPMR. Just like in sports, where your head goes, your body will follow.

The same applies to your professional development and self-mastery. Unleash your conscious and subconscious mind so that all of you is fully exerted on your goal, your natural filter system is engaged, and your conscious decisions allow you to achieve the best ROI for your time.

The EPMR is specifically designed so you review your goals first thing in the morning to align yourself. The secret benefit is that each morning, you take control on your way to one of six wins. The positive feeling is self-reinforcing. You don't simply wake up and react to what the world throws at you; you have a game plan and are the architect of it. This empowers you and provides you with that fortitude to drive through the ups and downs, all the while knowing, unequivocally, that you are in charge of your life, determining the destination you want to fly to. No plan ever takes off without a predetermined destination. As a pilot in command of your life, the same is true.

As you progress (and you will), this feeling of accomplishment, progress, mastering small details, or improvement will encourage you. Just like a pilot, sometimes you encounter weather or other acts of God that may require you to set new goals because circumstances changed. But then you plot a new course and choose a new destiny by taking all the knowledge and experience you gained on your previous journey that now has a new destination for your efforts. If you put your mind to anything you dream of, you can achieve it.

Step 3: Personal Accountability. The Right-Angle Rule unlocks your internal GPS. And through personal accountability, you will unequivocally reach your destination. This should be one of the most exciting and motivating aspects of the EPP™. You will arrive at your destiny if you (1) establish a positive mental attitude (PMA); (2) put your goals on a whiteboard, virtual or physical; and (3) hold yourself personally accountable by aligning your mental power with your clearly defined goal and then letting your built-in GPS allow your body to follow your head toward your visualized goal.

Michael Phelps once said, "If you want to be the best, you have to do things that other people aren't willing to do."[31] The difference between the top 5 percent and the rest of the 95 percent comes down to the same principle. When Michael Phelps was interviewed about his training, he was blunt and under no illusion. When waking up after a crushing defeat (yes, he had some), he did not want to train, but he made a simple decision to do so because he held himself personally accountable to the goal he set back at the age of nine years old to be the best Olympic swimmer he could be. "I can't remember the last day I didn't train,"[32] he said. Nike's slogan says it in a different way that has now become ubiquitous: "Just Do It."

Step 4: Positive Reinforcement. As it says in Proverbs, "One who has unreliable friends soon comes to ruin, but there is a friend who sticks closer than a brother."[33] Friends matter.

The best professional relationships feel like friendships. Aside from a significant other (who is likely to also be your best friend) or family members, your most important relationships are your friends. Make a conscious effort to surround yourself with like-minded people, those who respect

---

31 Michael Phelps Quotes, BrainyQuote.com, BrainyMedia Inc, accessed December 13, 2023, https://www.brainyquote.com/quotes/michael_phelps_440700.

32 Olivier Poirier-Leroy, "8 Michael Phelps Quotes to Get Your Fired Up," Swim Swam, July 1, 2016, https://swimswam.com/8-michael-phelps-quotes-get-fired/

33 Proverbs 18:24 (NIV)

you, support you, and believe in you. Associate yourself with the people who think you can. Do not expend energy on people who are skeptical or doubtful; instead, conserve that energy and fuel and apply it to the momentum you are building.

My favorite quote is by Theodore Roosevelt:

It is not the critic who counts; not the man who points out how the strong man stumbles, or where the doer of deeds could have done them better. The credit belongs to the man who is actually in the arena, whose face is marred by dust and sweat and blood; who strives valiantly; who errs, who comes short again and again, because there is no effort without error and shortcoming; but who does actually strive to do the deeds; who knows great enthusiasms, the great devotions; who spends himself in a worthy cause; who at the best knows in the end the triumph of high achievement, and who at the worst, if he fails, at least fails while daring greatly, so that his place shall never be with those cold and timid souls who neither know victory nor defeat.[34]

To begin with the end in mind is a technique that will enable you to make the absolute best of tomorrow, the first day of the rest of your life. This disciplined approach will take the God-given abilities that lie within you today, the innate attributes that enable you to perform a task, and channel this effort into the accomplishment of a clear goal. Led by your mind, your body will follow. It is your attitude and personal accountability that will enable you to perform at

34 The Roosevelt Center, "The Man in the Arena," Dickinson State University, accessed December 6, 2023, https://www.theodorerooseveltcenter.org/Learn-About-TR/TR-Encyclopedia/Culture-and-Society/Man-in-the-Arena.aspx.

an elite level, fully harvesting the inertia within yourself to passionately pursue the goals that you choose.

ADDITIONAL LIFE LESSONS

Some say art mimics life. As a passionate sports fan, I say life mimics sports. The good news is that you do not have to be a sports fan or athlete to benefit from these two life lessons I have learned.

The first is to maximize your sweet spot. Leverage your comfort zone and your growth zone. The sweet spot is the location at which the object being struck, usually a ball, absorbs the maximum amount of the available forward momentum and rebounds away from the racket, club, et cetera, with a greater velocity than if it were struck at any other point on the racket. This will result in more power transmitted to the ball. Likewise, as you progress on your journey to be elite, you will gain confidence in your inner self because it's based on a strong foundation of truth. Integrate this sweet spot into your personal tool kit.

To maximize your sweet spot, you have to know your sweet spot. Step into pitches when you see them coming. You have mastered the Right-Angle Rule. You know your strengths. So, when you see the opportunity to knock it out of the park, step up—carpe diem. When you are on the office tennis court, find the sweet spot that is aligned with your manager's goals, their manager's goals, and the firm's goals. Let them know that those are serves you can return every time. Own the strike zone and become a home run king. Elite performers reinforce their brand by owning their sweet spot and step it up a notch by expanding their comfort zone.

HOW TO EXPAND YOUR COMFORT ZONE

One of the key attributes of an elite performer is their ability to step from the comfort zone to the fear zone. According to an article from Positive Psychology, "In 1907, Robert Yerkes and John Dodson conducted one of the first experiments that illuminated a link between anxiety and performance. They saw that mice became more motivated to complete mazes when given electric shocks of increasing intensity—but only up to a point. Above a certain threshold, they began to hide rather than perform." The article furthermore states, "Corresponding behavior has been seen in human beings. This makes sense because, in response to anxiety-provoking stimuli, the options are either fight (meet the challenge), flight (run away/hide), or freeze (become paralyzed)."[35]

YERKES AND DODSON'S LAW

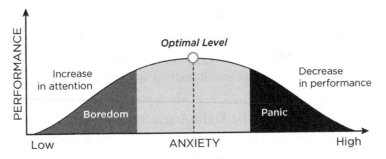

Find your optimal level and thrive.

It takes courage to step from the comfort zone into the fear zone. Without a clear roadmap, there's no way to build on previous experiences. This is the power of the Elite Performance Pillars™ you have embarked upon. You have a clear path, set by your internal GPS, so trust it. Continue and persevere on the path. By doing so, you enter the

35 Oliver Page, "How to Leave Your Comfort Zone and Enter Your 'Growth Zone,'" Positive Psychology, November 4, 2020, https://positivepsychology.com/comfort-zone/.

learning zone, where you gain new skills and deal with challenges resourcefully. After a learning period, a new comfort zone is created, expanding your ability to reach even greater heights. This is what it means to be in the growth zone.

While you move through this process of behavioral change, attempts into the growth zone will require a greater level of self-awareness; the Right-Angle Rule; and, ideally, a coach to help you perfect your technique of expanding your comfort zone along the way.

The second lesson I've learned as a sports fan is to be like water. The idea can help you stop yourself from feeling stuck. Yes, I've been there. You're stuck, perhaps in a confrontational relationship with a colleague, a failing project, or in a rut you can't get out of. I share this story with you in the hopes that next time you find yourself in this situation, you have an additional tool in your tool kit—the imagery of being like water.

In Managing Your Manager, we discussed the Art of Being Malleable. The epitome of being malleable is water in a liquid state. Early in my career, I had a mentor who shared my passion for martial arts and helped me understand that it can be easier during certain difficult encounters in life to be less rigid and more like water to overcome the impasse.

Bruce Lee was not only a master of martial arts but a philosophical thinker who gave much thought to life and how it should be lived—an early graduate of the EPP™! Lee voiced his life and martial arts philosophies with many famous quotes such as, "Be like water."[36] What does this statement actually mean? Lee's quote about being like water referred to his approach to martial arts and life in general. Water adapts and changes to its surroundings and obstacles,

36 Dushyant, "'Be Like Water' – What Did Bruce Lee Mean?" Catalyst, accessed December 6, 2023, https://catalystinspired.com/be-like-water-by-bruce-lee/.

but when water comes with power, it is an unstoppable, irresistible force that little can withstand.

In Lee's philosophy, the martial artist should be like water, formless and shapeless. This means that the martial artist should be able to adapt to any situation and flow with the opponent's attacks. Lee believed that the human body is naturally designed to move fluidly and efficiently. According to Lee, being like water meant being flexible, adaptable, and resilient. He said that water has no shape, but it can take any form depending on the container it is in. He also said that water can flow gently or crash violently, depending on the situation. He wanted to apply these principles to his fighting style and his mindset so that he could overcome any obstacle or opponent. [37]

Think about this in a business context. Being like water could mean being able to adjust to different situations, markets, customers, competitors, and challenges. It could also mean being creative and innovative, finding new ways to solve problems or create value. It could also mean being resilient and persistent, not giving up easily or being discouraged by failures.

For me, it is an image that I use when I do not know how to proceed. Water always finds its way to the lowest point. It pursues the path of least resistance. It is an internal prompt I use to step back and explore different options, asking myself if I am missing the obvious next step because my emotions are heightened and my thoughts unclear.

Lee believed that we should be adaptable and fluid in our actions but also have the serenity and strength that water possesses. When we are "like water," we can flow through

37 Neod, "Be Like Water—Meaning and Wisdom Of Bruce Lee's Philosophy," Comanifesting, accessed November 19, 2023, https://comanifesting.com/be-like-water-meaning/.

life's challenges with ease and grace. So, the next time you find yourself stuck, frustrated, or in a rut, "be like water."

The principle of being like water is incorporated into Elite Performance Pillar™ III: Managing your Manager in being malleable to your manager's needs. Your willingness to adapt and bend (like water) your schedule to your manager's needs will strengthen your relationship and make you an asset.

CHAPTER 13 **TAKEAWAYS**

- Succeeding in the Elite Performance Pillars™ program requires self-accountability. Be true to yourself throughout the journey by accepting your weaknesses and owning your strengths. Take comfort in this: there is only one amazing you on the planet. That's how The Creator planned it.

- The four steps to help you on your EPP™ journey are:
    - Step 1: PMA—always maintain a positive mental attitude.
    - Step 2: set whiteboard goals.
    - Step 3: maintain personal accountability.
    - Step 4: use positive reinforcement (Proverbs 18:24).

- Additional life lessons:
    - Maximize your sweet spot; leverage your comfort zone and your growth zone.
    - Stop yourself from feeling stuck by being like water.

GO AFTER THE CAREER YOU DESIRE AND THE LIFE YOU DESERVE!

"If you believe in yourself and have dedication and pride—and never quit, you'll be a winner. The price of victory is high but so are the rewards."
—BEAR BRYANT

NOW IS YOUR TIME to ascend. It's your time to follow your internal GPS and go after the career you desire and the life you deserve. Many people aspire to reach their goals and live the life they have always dreamed of. However, you've taken the critical step and put your improved foundation into practice over the last several weeks. Now, you have your own elite performance morning routine and you're building a better you (Pillar I) by investing in yourself every day.

You have created momentum with your brand, and you are committed to being a better manager (Pillar II) by managing your team with an increased level of self-awareness. A new dynamic is forming within your team as you first ask your team members where they would like to lean in—which fosters their sense of ownership—and then manage the mission by matching the tasks to the individuals' strengths, passions, and values. Formal one-on-one meetings are now booked on the calendar, but the focus is on active listening and coaching through stories versus telling. You know Jekyll and Hyde don't exist, so your professional standard for one-on-ones has no compromise. Start on time.

Don't reschedule. Be there to help. But in return, your reports must increase their own level of self-awareness.

Managing your manager (Pillar 3), which encompasses the Push and Pull Rule, starts with you pushing hard in everything you do to help your boss succeed. In doing so, you help create a positive correlation, allowing them to pull you forward, following their slipstream.

Aesop's fable of "The Oak and the Reed" shares a lesson about humility and adaptability. It teaches that a small reed that bends in the wind is stronger than a mighty oak tree that can break in a storm.[38] This lesson reminds us to be malleable, suggesting that being able to bend with the changing circumstances is a better strategy than being rigid and stubborn. There will be those times when we hit an unforgiving wall or find ourselves stuck, and that is when we need to "be like water," inspired by Bruce Lee. Adapt and change to your surroundings and flow through the challenge with ease and grace.

You have learned to reserve judgment regarding management's decisions, having realized information can be asymmetric and that, sometimes, you just need to give your boss a break. They will appreciate it.

Being an elite performer takes dedication, resilience, and unwavering determination to consistently improve step by step, striving toward excellence. It requires the willingness to put in the hard work toward your FAST objectives, commit to your daily EPMR, and constantly test your limits.

It also entails maximizing your sweet spot by leveraging the expansion of your comfort zone into a growth zone. Moving into the growth zone by overcoming the anxiety of flight requires increased self-awareness and, ideally, a coach to help perfect your technique along the way.

38 Aesop and Michael Hague, *Aesop's Fables*. New York, Henry Holt, 1985.

To accomplish these aspirations, you have been given the Elite Performance Pillars™ framework. You need to understand that it requires daily discipline and a consistent work ethic to achieve the success of an elite performer. Having an elite mindset means having the discipline of an athlete and the focus of a chief executive officer.

CHAPTER 14 **TAKEAWAYS**

- It's time to follow your internal GPS and go after the career you desire and the life you deserve.

- You have created momentum with your brand, and you are committed to being a better manager (Pillar II) by managing your team with an increased level of self-awareness.

- There will be those times when you hit an unforgiving wall. That is when you need to "be like water," inspired by Bruce Lee. Adapt and change to your surroundings, and flow through the challenge with ease and grace.

- To accomplish these aspirations, you have been given the Elite Performance Pillars™ framework. You need to understand that it requires daily discipline and a consistent work ethic to achieve the success of an elite performer.

PART VI

WORKING WITH EXECPATHFINDERS LLC

GET IN THE ARENA!
TAKE ACTION TODAY!

*"Success is not final; failure is not fatal. It is the courage
to continue that counts."*

—WINSTON CHURCHILL

THE FIRST DAY of the rest of your life starts today. Do not waste it. With self-application, the EPP™ framework provided in this book can be the best career guide you have ever had. Mark today on the calendar as the day you commit to becoming an elite performer. Find an ally, mentor, or executive coach and tell them that you are embarking on the ExecPathfinders program to become an elite performer and to have the career you've always desired and the joy you have always deserved.

In my executive coaching program, ExecPathfinders LLC, I work daily with elite performers who have fully embraced the Elite Performance Pillars™, and it has revolutionized their lives. This book contains direct links to the ExecPathfinders website (*www.ExecPathfinders.com*) to help support you on every step of your journey. We understand that your time is valuable, and that's why we offer a range of coaching programs at ExecPathfinders. Our programs are designed to cater to your specific needs, whether you prefer online, interactive multimedia training, or custom-tailored individual coaching programs. These highly effective programs are specifically designed to help accelerate the implementation of the three core principles of the Elite Performance Pillars™ so your career can immediately start to benefit from the proven methodology underpinning the program.

It's now your turn to step into the arena and take action in your career. If you never invest the time to manage your career, you can never grow. You now know that what separates the elite performers, the top 5 percent, is doing what the other 95 percent are unwilling to do. It starts with committing 5–10 percent of your time every week to planning your career. This simple act of taking ownership of managing your career will make a world of difference. After all, if you're not managing it, then who is? Your life's work deserves careful consideration. Take intentional steps to align with your goals and values for maximum impact.

Here's where career coaching enters the picture. As an expert in the field, a career coach understands the limitations of organizations when it comes to career development. They provide the missing piece—the personalized guidance, strategies, and ongoing support that organizations can't often offer. A career coach becomes your partner in crafting a tailored plan, navigating challenges, and seizing opportunities that align with your unique ambitions.

This is exactly the kind of coaching with which I support my clients to help them take charge of their journey and put them back in the driver's seat of their own careers. By embracing self-management and seeking the guidance of a trusted career coach, you will break free from the false notion that your company will handle your career growth.

Be mindful of coaches employed by your firm. They are employed to help the company accomplish its goals, which may not always be aligned with your personal growth and career objectives, thereby creating an inherent conflict of interest. Furthermore, there's a confidentiality issue. Unless you have specific assurance that the coach's observations and feedback will not go back to the firm's management, it will be difficult for you to discuss your personal weaknesses or concerns regarding the firm, knowing that they could ultimately be shared with your management.

In essence, to progress in the journey ahead, you must acknowledge that no one knows your dreams, strengths, and aspirations better than you. With dedication and the right support, you can proactively shape your professional trajectory, leveraging your potential for success and fulfillment.

Embrace the fact that your career development rests in your hands. Seek the assistance of a career coach who is solely aligned with your success, understands the limitations of corporate settings, and can help you navigate the complexities. An executive career coach who is directly aligned with your career development can bridge the gap that organizations simply cannot fill.

If you would like some help along the way, reading this book to completion is your very first step. The counsel and personalized insights I offer hold exceptional significance because they present a perspective that is truly unparalleled. Such guidance is notably absent in conventional HR programs or standard management courses, making this unique vantage point an extraordinary resource that cannot be found elsewhere. Rest assured, the knowledge and wisdom I provide are bound to enrich your understanding in ways that transcend traditional avenues of career development.

Earlier in the book, we discussed how I enjoyed working with a health care executive client who came to me with a thriving business. He was the founder and CEO and had the ambition to grow the top line by tenfold. He sought my services to help him develop a growth strategy to achieve his goal. The first task I asked him to do was to record how he spent every thirty minutes of each day for one week. During our next executive coaching session, we reviewed how he spent his time. This simple exercise was very revealing for him. He's a very talented businessperson who is ethically grounded and truly cares immensely about patient care and the responsibility that was bestowed on his firm. Because of his passion, he took on the primary responsibility to personally follow up with new patient introductions, was hands-on with the financials, and was sensitive to maintaining direct reporting relationships, even as the firm grew beyond one hundred employees.

We discussed the importance of ring-fencing 5–10 percent of his time so he could manage his career and act as the CEO, working with me to develop a growth strategy to achieve his target. What transpired was a definitive turning point for his business.

He realized that he could not think strategically as the CEO if he was not committing 5–10 percent of his time on a weekly basis to do so. We then took action together. He empowered a recent senior sales hire to be responsible for the primary follow-up for all new patient referrals and asked them to only involve the founder on an exceptional basis that met certain criteria. He consolidated reporting lines and further empowered his head of human resources to update all employees' roles and responsibilities and check in on employee morale throughout the process. He had his executive assistant systematically block out three hours a week that he dedicated to managing his career as CEO and founder (his executive coaching sessions represented one hour per week). For the first time, he unplugged, did not take calls, and had the opportunity to apply critical thinking to determine which client segments could underpin his ambitious growth targets. This also created time for him to think about potential acquisitions and meet with bankers and consultants to discuss industry trends and benchmarks.

He committed 5–10 percent of his time to managing his career, and it profoundly changed the trajectory of his firm. It will have the same impact on your career if you commit the time consistently.

Most importantly, you don't have to do it alone. Every single person should be guided by a trusted mentor or coach. The value of coaching is that it can accelerate your career growth in a fraction of the time. I've learned from mentors throughout my career that the benefit of coaching is that you can formalize what was informal before.

CHAPTER 15 **TAKEAWAYS**

- The first day of the rest of your life starts to-day.

- A career coach is solely aligned with your success and becomes your partner in crafting a tailored plan, navigating challenges, and seizing opportunities that align with your unique ambitions.

- ExecPathfinders LLC's highly effective coaching programs are specifically designed to help accelerate the implementation of the three Elite Performance Pillars™ core principles so your career can immediately start to benefit from the proven methodology underpinning the program.

- Find out more about ExecPathfinders LLC's services at www.ExecPathfinders.com.

INCEPTURI SUMUS

"One day or day one. You decide."

—PAULO COELHO

NCEPTURI SUMUS is a Latin expression that implies a sense of readiness and determination to start something new. As you embark upon this new chapter of your life, it is with immense gratitude that I say thank you for reading this book, and for trusting me on your journey ahead.

I have done my utmost to codify the lessons I have learned into a methodology covering the three core pillars of your career. My goal is to provide you with the insights and unspoken tools I have acquired over a forty-year career, distilled into a simple step-by-step guide that you can use to revolutionize your current mode of operation and start enjoying success in your career every day you wake up.

The journey has begun. You have invested in your personal tool kit. You have changed your habits, which will change your life. You are the pilot in command of you. Remember, life has two kinds of people: those who think they can, and those who think they can't, and they are both right. You and I know who you are. You wouldn't have made it this far in the book if you did not believe you could! However, your career won't grow itself, and your firm won't grow it for you. That is why you need an executive career coach today, not tomorrow.

What is an executive coach, anyway? An executive coach is a professional who works one-on-one with executives to help them improve their skills, achieve their goals, and accelerate their careers. The coach provides unbiased feedback, guidance, and support to help the client over-come challenges, make better decisions, and develop the leadership qualities necessary to succeed.

We like to model ourselves after excellence at ExecPath-finders. Our coaches work directly for the individual client under a bilateral confidentiality agreement, ensuring there is no conflict of interest. Whatever is discussed stays strictly between the coach and the client. No information is ever shared with any outside parties—not your employer, not your manager, and not your human resources department. We work only for you, and we are completely aligned with your holistic success on a strictly confidential basis.

Perhaps no one has said what a coach is better than Tom Landry: "A coach is someone who tells you what you don't want to hear, who has you see what you don't want to see, so you can be who you have always known you could be."[39] (We liked this so much we have it on our website!)

Here are some ways an executive coach can help accelerate your career and why you need one:

1. Improve yourself by raising your self-awareness: An executive coach can help you identify your strengths, weaknesses, and blind spots, allowing you to develop a more accurate self-assessment of your skills and abilities. This can help you make better decisions, communicate more effectively, and improve your leadership style.

2. Set clearer FAST goals: At ExecPathfinders, we use FAST methodology to help set clearer and more specific career goals, allowing you to focus your efforts

---

39 Tom Landry Quotes, AZ Quotes, accessed December 6, 2023, https://www.azquotes.com/author/8459-Tom_Landry.

and achieve better results. This can include identifying your long-term goals; breaking them down into smaller, achievable steps; and creating a roadmap to success.

3. Enhance your management and leadership skills: An executive coach can help you develop the specific leadership skills you need to succeed in your role, such as clear communication via your commander's intent, improved collaboration, and the substitution of inclusion for delegation. By improving these skills, you can become a more effective manager, build stronger relationships with your team, and inspire greater productivity and engagement.

4. Navigate complex situations: An executive coach can offer guidance and support as you navigate complex and challenging situations in your career, such as difficult conversations, conflicts, and crises. With a coach's help, you can develop strategies to manage these situations effectively, maintain your composure, and stay focused on your goals.

5. Manage your manager to accelerate your career growth: An executive coach can provide you with the interpersonal tools, strategies (like push and pull), and advisory support to help you accelerate your career growth, whether that means pursuing new opportunities, developing new skills, or taking on more challenging assignments. With a coach's help, you can develop a clear action plan to achieve your career objectives and build the influence and visibility you need to succeed.

The journey isn't for everyone, but only for those who are willing to face themselves; work hard; learn; be open-minded; and experience growth, excellence, and success. We work with rising talents, experienced managers, and executives seeking to compete at the elite levels of their industry, elite performers who can handle stress, pressure, setbacks, and adversity and remain focused and resilient.

Moreover, we are passionate and purposeful about what we do. We seek those clients who have a deep love and enthusiasm for what they do and a shared sense that what we accomplish together has meaning and fulfillment that goes beyond external rewards.

In conclusion, an executive coach can help accelerate the implementation of the journey you have just begun, enabling you to become an elite performer in the industry of your choice in a compressed time period. At the elite level, it gives you the chessboard advantage: the coach actively listens, observes, and can offer a different perspective, one unaffected by being "in the game." They can see all the chess pieces all the time because they have the luxury of not being on the board, and they work directly for you. With a coach's support and guidance, you can achieve your goals faster, build stronger relationships, and become a more confident and effective leader. To put it simply, if you want to be better at whatever you do, get a coach.

For coaching, mentoring, and support to accelerate your journey to become an elite performer in your industry, please go to my website, www.ExecPathfinders.com, or send us an email at *ExecPathfinders@gmail.com*

CHAPTER 16 **TAKEAWAYS**

- The journey has begun. You have invested in your personal tool kit. You have changed your habits, which will change your life, and you are the pilot in command of you. However, your career won't grow itself, and your company won't grow it for you. That's why you need an executive career coach today, not tomorrow.

- A coach will tell you what you don't want to hear and see what you don't want to see so they can help you be who you have always known you could be.

- Please check out *www.ExecPathfinders.com* to learn how we can help accelerate your career so you can achieve the happiness and success you deserve.

WOULD YOU LIKE A BONUS CHAPTER?

Thank you for investing your time in reading my book and taking the first step toward becoming an elite performer. As a token of my appreciation, I have included a bonus chapter on my website that delves deeper into "The Paradox: How Experience can Impair Judgment." In this chapter, I share a profound personal experience that has left a lasting impression on my life and the valuable lesson I learned from it. I am confident that this lesson can become a part of your personal tool kit as well. So, head over to my website to check out the bonus chapter, and take another step toward becoming an elite performer.

Please find the bonus chapter at:

ACKNOWLEDGMENTS

I WILL BE FOREVER grateful to Ashley Mansour for her transformative Book Accelerator program, underscored by her innovative TAP Method. The exceptional personal coaching, unwavering support, and invaluable encouragement extended by Ashley and her team of experts—coach Jess; coach Melody; my project manager, Chelsea; and my editor, Jan—played a pivotal role in translating my aspiration of crafting a career guidebook into a tangible reality. Their guidance was instrumental in bringing forth my vision to empower others.

In parallel, I am grateful for the privilege of learning and growing through the guidance and support of exceptional institutions, including the US Army, the University of Wisconsin–Madison, and the University of Cambridge Judge Business School. Additionally, I owe a debt of gratitude to the remarkable organizations that contributed to my professional development, namely IBM, Hewlett-Packard, JP Morgan, Lehman Brothers Inc., and BNP Paribas. Throughout my tenure at these esteemed institutions, I had the privilege of working alongside exceptional mentors, managers, and colleagues whose invaluable lessons have indelibly shaped my growth and success.

My dear friend Colin MacIntosh deserves my heartfelt gratitude for his encouragement, which was the spark that ignited my passion to share my career management insights in a book. His motivation inspired me to encapsulate my unique perspective, drawing upon the best lessons I learned from my military service and my time in international finance. I am grateful for his valuable input and support throughout the journey of writing this book.

To my supportive sisters, esteemed brothers-in-law, and close circle of friends, I sincerely thank you for your unwavering encouragement from the outset. A special acknowledgment goes to retired US Army Lieutenant Colonel Donald M. Wix, a dear confidant and exemplar of dedication, honor, and duty. His invaluable insights and guidance ensured the accuracy and potency of my military analogies, allowing me to effectively convey the intended key messages.

My amazing wife deserves my deepest gratitude for her unwavering support throughout this journey. She stood by me through countless hours spent at my computer and engaged in Zoom discussions. My heartfelt thanks also go to my sons, whose unwavering support provided the backbone for the realization of this endeavor. The completion of this book stands as a testament to the collective commitment of those who have enriched my journey, and for that, I am profoundly thankful.

BIBLIOGRAPHY

1   Gladwell, Malcolm. *Outliers*. Penguin UK, 2008.

2   Shaw, George Bernard. *Man and Superman*. Penguin, 1903.

3   Suzanne Kane, "How to Be Honest With Yourself," Psych Central, last modified August 19, 2017, *https://psychcentral.com/blog/how-to-be-honest-with-yourself*.

4   Christopher D. Connors, "Honesty—How it Benefits You and Others," Medium, September 7, 2016, *https://medium.com/the-mission/honesty-how-it-benefits-you-and-others-ecb3e7fabb9a*.

5   MacArthur, General Douglas. "Duty, Honor, Country." Address at West Point Military Academy, New York, May 12, 1962.

6   UT News, "Adm. McRaven Urges Graduates to Find Courage to Save the World," The University of Texas at Austin, May 16, 2014, *https://news.utexas.edu/2014/05/16/mcraven-urges-graduates-to-find-courage-to-change-the-world/*.

7   Danielle Pacheco and Abhinav Singh, "Sleep Calculator: Your Personalized Tool for Sleep," Sleep Foundation, accessed November 12, 2023, *https://www.sleepfoundation.org/sleep-calculator*.

8   Maltz, Maxwell. *Psycho-Cybernetics: Updated and Expanded.* TarcherPerigree, 2015.

9   UCL, "How long does it take to form a habit?" University College London, August 4, 2009, *https://www.ucl.ac.uk/news/2009/aug/how-long-does-it-take-form-habit.*

10 Donald Sull and Charles Sull, "With Goals, FAST Beats SMART," MIT Sloan Management Review, June 5, 2018, https://sloanreview.mit.edu/article/with-goals-fast-beats-smart/; Steve Preda and Gregory Cleary, *Pinnacle.*

11 Pink, Daniel H. *When: The Scientific Secrets of Perfect Timing.* Penguin, 2018.

12 Marie Doorey, "George A. Miller," *Encyclopedia Brittanica*, July 18, 2023, *https://www.britannica.com/biography/George-A-Miller#ref1200615.*

13 Rhett Power, "How to Focus Like George Lucas," *Forbes*, May 3, 2020, *https://www.forbes.com/sites/rhettpower/2020/05/03/how-to-focus-like-george-lucas/?sh=73a5b8f1510b.*

14 Von Clausewitz, Carl. *Principles of War.* Courier Corporation, 2012.

15 Chad Storlie, "Manage Uncertainty with Commander's Intent," Harvard Business Review, November 3, 2010, *https://hbr.org/2010/11/dont-play-golf-in-a-football-g.*

16 Whitmore, John. *Coaching for Performance.*
    Nicholas Brealy Publishing, 2009.

17 Covey, Stephen R. *The 7 Habits of Highly Effective
    People: Powerful Lessons in Personal Change.* Free
    Press, 2004.

18 Winston S. Churchill, "An hour [of] Preparation
    for Each Minute [of] Delivery," Finest Hour,
    International Churchill Society, September
    5, 2013, *https://winstonchurchill.org/
    publications/finest-hour/finest-hour-106/
    winston-churchill-author-and-historian/.*

19 History Extra, "8 of Churchill's greatest speeches,"
    BBC History Magazine, November 24, 2021, *https://
    www.historyextra.com/period/second-world-war/
    churchills-greatest-speeches/*

20 Kozlowski, Steve W. J. and Bradford S. Bell. *Work
    Groups and Teams in Organizations.* John Wiley &
    Sons, Inc., 2003.

21 Heleen Van Mierlo and Edwin A. J. Van Hooft, "Team
    Achievement Goals and Sports Team Performance,"
    Sage Publishing, 2020, *https://journals.sagepub.
    com/doi/pdf/10.1177/1046496420913119.*

22 Logan Nye, "The SEAL behind the '40 percent rule' is
    a fitness beast," We Are the Mighty, October 6, 2022,
    *https://www.wearethemighty.com/mighty-fit/
    navy-seal-40-percent-rule/.*

23 Flavia Medrut, "Michael Jordan's Most Powerful Life Lessons for When You Feel Like a Failure," Goalcast, accessed December 6, 2023, *https://www.goalcast. com/michael-jordan-life-lessons-on-failure/*.

24 Mandela, Nelson. *Long Walk to Freedom*. Little Brown & Co., 1994.

25 The Art of Service. *Hoshin Kanri A Complete Guide*. Hoshin Kanri Publishing, 2020.

26 Sharma, Robin. *The 5AM Club: Own Your Morning. Elevate Your Life*. Harpercollins Publishers, 2018.

27 Kenneth Abramowitz, "General MacArthur's Speech to Cadets at the U.S. Military Academy, 1962," Save the West, May 25, 2020, *https://savethewest.com/ douglas-macarthurs-speech-to-cadets-at-the-u-s-military-academy-1962/*.

28 Marty Nemko Ph.D., "The Power of Mirroring," *Psychology Today*, October 31, 2021, *https://www. psychologytoday.com/us/blog/how-do-life/202110/ the-power-mirroring*.

29 Mark Synnott, "Exclusive: Alex Honnold Completes the Most Dangerous Free-Solo Event Ever," *National Geographic,* October 3, 2018, *https://www. nationalgeographic.com/adventure/article/most-dangerous-free-solo-climb-yosemite-national-park-el-capitan*.

30 Quoteresearch, "Whether You Believe You Can Do a Thing or Not, You Are Right," Quote Investigator, February 3, 2015, *https://quoteinvestigator. com/2015/02/03/you-can/*.

31 Michael Phelps Quotes, BrainyQuote.com, BrainyMedia Inc, accessed December 13, 2023, *https://www.brainyquote.com/quotes/ michael_phelps_440700*.

32 Olivier Poirier-Leroy, "8 Michael Phelps Quotes to Get Your Fired Up," Swim Swam, July 1, 2016, *https:// swimswam.com/8-michael-phelps-quotes-get-fired/*.

33 Proverbs 18:24 (NIV)

34 The Roosevelt Center, "The Man in the Arena," Dickinson State University, accessed December 6, 2023, *https://www.theodorerooseveltcenter.org/ Learn-About-TR/TR-Encyclopedia/Culture-and-Society/Man-in-the-Arena.aspx*.

35 Oliver Page, "How to Leave Your Comfort Zone and Enter Your 'Growth Zone,'" Positive Psychology, November 4, 2020, *https://positivepsychology.com/ comfort-zone/*.

36 Dushyant, "'Be Like Water' – What Did Bruce Lee Mean?" Catalyst, accessed December 6, 2023, *https:// catalystinspired.com/be-like-water-by-bruce-lee/*.

37 Neod, "Be Like Water—Meaning and Wisdom Of
    Bruce Lee's Philosophy," Comanifesting, accessed
    November 19, 2023, *https://comanifesting.com/
    be-like-water-meaning/*.

38 Aesop and Michael Hague, *Aesop's Fables*. New York,
    Henry Holt, 1985.

39 Tom Landry Quotes, AZ Quotes, accessed
    December 6, 2023, *https://www.azquotes.com/
    author/8459-Tom_Landry*.

With three decades of experience in international finance, Talbot Stark is the visionary founder and CEO of ExecPathfinders. ExecPathfinders stands as a beacon of transformation in the realm of executive coaching, extending its reach across the global stage. Through its proprietary Elite Performance Pillars™ methodology, this pioneering firm catalyzes profound change, nurturing senior professionals in reshaping their minds, careers, and destinies.

ExecPathfinders' innovative approach is more than just a coaching regimen; the firm crafts a holistic framework that not only reshapes individual trajectories but also permeates organizational cultures. Talbot's work in executive coaching and strategy consulting creates a unique blend of strategic acumen honed from a seasoned finance career and combat arms leadership from the US Army's aviation branch.

Talbot's personal mission resonates with unwavering passion: to illuminate the path of elite performers, igniting a transformative journey toward the happiness and success they deserve. With a strong commitment to helping others, he tirelessly shares the invaluable fruits of his experience, offering a guiding beacon to navigate the intricate landscapes of achievement. Talbot's academic accomplishments include a CFA, an MBA from the University of Cambridge Judge Business School, and a BS in Industrial Engineering from the University of Wisconsin–Madison.

For more information on Talbot Stark and ExecPathfinders, please visit *www.ExecPathfinders.com*.

Made in the USA
Middletown, DE
14 February 2024

49670961R00136